THE STORY TO
TABLE MESA

"FROM THE CRUMBS BENEATH THE TABLE TO A SEAT AT THE TABLE"

A BOOK FOR ENTREPRENEURS, RESTAURATEURS, FAITH JOURNEY ADVENTURES, MEMOIR READERS, AND SELF-HELP FINE-TUNING.

CARL BYRON GARRETT

ISBN: 979-8-89694-184-2 - Paperback
ISBN: 979-8-89694-183-5 - eBook
ISBN: 979-8-89694-185-9 - Hardcover

DEDICATION

I dedicate this book to my mother, Marjorie, whose love was boundless and whose generosity inspired me beyond measure—may God bless her for all eternity. Through her struggles, she taught me the meaning of grace and kindness, and her legacy lives on in everything I do.

ACKNOWLEDGMENTS

First and foremost, I want to acknowledge my loving wife and business partner, Lindie. She has been my anchor and unwavering support on this journey of faith. Her encouragement, wisdom, and partnership have been vital in both my spiritual walk and our entrepreneurial ventures. Without her, this achievement would not have been possible.

I'm also deeply grateful to Fernanda Fulkerson, a dear friend and a brilliant culinary collaborator. Fernanda's creativity has been instrumental in shaping Table Mesa, Tavola, and the other culinary concepts we've brought to life together.

To our youngest daughter, my sweet and talented muse: your gifts and creativity have enriched not only the cover of this book but the vision behind so much of what we do. You remind me daily of the joy of dreaming big.

To my daughters in Houston, who stood beside me through the middle chapters of my life, thank you. Your love, faith, and encouragement have been a steady source of strength and hope.

To my cousin Nicki, who has been like a sister to me. Her knowledge and camaraderie have been a constant gift throughout the years, and I am deeply grateful for her presence in my life.

I would like to express my sincere gratitude to Andres Sommer for his invaluable contributions over the past 20 years in helping to establish our brands in Seattle and Northwest Arkansas. His exceptional talent as a graphic artist and master web designer—evident in our menus, websites, and logos—has played a pivotal role in setting us apart. His creativity and expertise have been instrumental in shaping our brand identity, and I am truly grateful for his partnership.

To all our wonderful staff who have made the trek with us on this restaurant journey, your hard work and loyalty never go unnoticed, and there is never a lack of appreciation.

Above all, I give thanks to my heavenly Father and His Son, Jesus Christ. In my darkest moments, they rescued me. Through every step, they've been faithful, never abandoning me, always pouring out love and grace. Without them, none of this would exist, for they are the source of all that I am and all that I have.

FORWARD

My husband, Dick, and I have known Carl and Lindie for over 15 years. In fact, when Carl and Lindie had their baby girl, they came to us and said, "H. has no grandparent influence in her life, and we are officially adopting you as grandparents for H." Needless to say, we have taken our job very seriously. We have "grandma days," we travel together, and we are present for most of her dedicated events. As one can see, we have become family.

The book itself is an extraordinary read about a young boy who was basically left to raise himself. Even though his mother loved him dearly, she had her own mental struggles. In spite of the circumstances, God had His hands on Carl, teaching and leading him into His plan, even when he was unaware of it.

From Carl's salvation, as a long-haired surfer, in the back of a pick-up truck, he has become a phenomenally successful restaurateur who trusts His God and Savior. This man started with nothing, faced many arduous situations, and has expanded to own seven restaurants and still counting.

When Carl maneuvers the obstacles of opening a new restaurant, he flourishes in the creativity and chaos of bringing the job to fruition. In other words, he is operating in his God given gifts and talents.

When Carl started serving the Lord, he began to know (1) God was real. (2) God had always been there for him all along. (3) God had a plan that only he could fulfill. [God has a plan for each one of us. After all, He knew us before we were in our mother's womb. *Isa.44:2*]

As you read The Story to Table Mesa "From the Crumbs Beneath the Table to a Seat at the Table", *you will be inspired with hope, resilience, seeds of faith, and reliance on God in order to fulfill God's plan for* **your** *life. Your faith will grow knowing that you have a story as well.*

> *For I am convinced of this very thing that*
> *he who began a good work in you will*
> *perfect it until the day of Christ Jesus.*
> *Philippians 1:6 NASB*

Shelley Perry - Retired School Principal

CONTENTS

CHAPTER 1

Fresh Bread

C hildhood often feels like a canvas of vivid memories, but mine was painted with shades of insecurity and struggle. While others might recall carefree days, I grew up navigating a world of uncertainty—one that tested my resilience and shaped the person I would become. I was born in Washington, DC in 1956, right amid the baby boomer generation.

Most of my memories from that time are filled with cold Winters, with a few Falls and Summers sprinkled in. Spring in Washington, DC, is easily the best season, in my opinion, thanks to the stunning cherry blossoms along the Potomac River, a welcome change from the frigid winter months.

As an inner-city kid, my days were spent playing in Rock Creek Park, and hide-and-seek in back alleys, dodging cars on our bikes, and riding the DC Metro buses to places like the zoo, the Georgetown pool in summer, and the local movie theaters. The Savoy and Tivoli theaters, with their balcony seating and giant screens, were some of the best. That was life in Washington in those days. As an only child, my interactions were mostly with adults, as my single mother raised me.

From ages four to eight, my life was a blur of constant moves. Basement apartments on Calvert Street and weekly-rented hotels became a revolving backdrop to our existence. Each time the rent came due, we'd pack up again, my mother's job struggles forcing us into this endless cycle. Once, we, or I should say I, landed in Junior Village, an orphanage for abandoned children. It was a cold, institutional place that etched itself into my memory. My mother, though loving, was in an uphill battle with life, moving from one unstable job to the next. I didn't realize it at the time, but those years taught me resilience—a lesson that would shape my future.

My mother took whatever jobs she could find, but "broke" was a constant theme in our lives. I remember her working as a housekeeper at the Ritz Carlton, often from 6:00 p.m. until early morning. I was terrified of being left alone in our tiny, dark apartment. One day, while riding my bike, I found a crisp one-dollar bill on the sidewalk and raced home, hoping it would be enough for her to take the night off so we could enjoy a BBQ pulled pork sandwich and Coke at Rexall Drugs, our go-to spot. But unfortunately, that dollar didn't stretch far enough, and she left for work as usual. She always read to me before she left, hoping I'd fall asleep; she'd kiss my forehead and whisper, "Dream of better days, my love." That small gesture felt like a promise she couldn't always keep, but as soon as the door locked behind her, my eyes would pop open, and I'd be wide awake, alone and scared.

Our little basement apartment was filled with shadows that cast scary figures on the walls, and I was more frightened of what was inside than what was outside. I would often unlock the door and leave the lights on, just in case I needed to make a quick escape from whatever I imagined was lurking inside.

We eventually moved again, with little more than the clothes on our backs. One evening, as we passed the Washington DC Cathedral, my mother spoke of guardian angels and suggested we go inside. "Let's light a candle," she said, "and say a prayer." I didn't know much about angels or God, but a quiet peace in that moment brought me comfort. Back then, I knew the Lord's Prayer from first grade, and it's stayed with me ever since. Somewhere along the way, I was given a small pocket-sized Bible, and I knew instinctively it was something special. I slept with it under my pillow, and that night I prayed for a home and a car—simple things I deeply longed for.

My mother's emotional and mental instability often led to unpredictable outbursts. She would lash out at strangers, accusing them of giving her a dirty look, leaving me feeling embarrassed and wishing I could disappear. Yet, when she wasn't battling her inner struggles, she could be incredibly sweet.

Our situation didn't go unnoticed. Social workers eventually stepped in, leading to court visits and, sometimes, stays at Junior Village while they evaluated my mother's condition. Being separated from her was heartbreaking, and I couldn't shake the feeling that somehow it was my fault.

I remember a day at school when the police arrived at the principal's office. The principal and another woman came into my class, speaking softly to my third-grade teacher. I couldn't shake the feeling that it was about me. All the students were curious about why the principal was talking to our teacher, whispering, "Who's in trouble?" I stayed silent.

When my teacher called me to her desk, her soft words, "Follow these people; it will be all right," did little to calm the storm rising in my stomach. As tears welled up, I glanced back at my classmates, their curious stares piercing my embarrassment. A little girl in the front row began to cry, and I felt a lump in my throat. Minutes later, I found myself ushered into the back of a police car, my world shifting in ways I couldn't yet understand. This was my initiation into a new chapter of struggle—Junior Village.

"Where's my mom?" I asked. "She's okay," the officer replied. "We're going to take you to a place where you'll have to stay for a while." I thought, *This is what it feels like to be a prisoner.* The officers were kind and offered to turn on the siren, which helped distract me from where I was heading.

CHAPTER 2

The Orphanage and the Struggle

Junior Village wasn't just bleak—it was unforgiving. The kind of place that wore you down, where the tears of forgotten children fell like rain. Most of the kids were Black. I was one of the few white ones, and while I might've stood out for that reason, but what really set us all apart from the outside world was our shared loneliness. It wrapped around us, binding us in ways we didn't fully understand.

The days were tense, filled with fights and tests of will— unspoken battles that became the currency of survival. During my first week, I noticed a couple of white kids sitting together in the cafeteria. I thought, maybe naively, that they'd welcome me. We looked alike, didn't we? That had to count for something. But when I approached, one of them glanced up and said, "What do you want, white boy?" The words hit me harder than I expected.

"Aren't you white?" I asked, confused. They just returned to their conversation, shutting me out like I wasn't even there.

That moment lingered—not because of their rejection, but if they weren't claiming the identity the world handed them, then why should I? Maybe the lines society draws between us didn't mean much there. Slowly, I began to see that what mattered wasn't race—it was the shared weight we all carried—the loneliness of being left behind.

I adapted quickly because I had to. In a place like Junior Village, survival was everything. I started to make friends, not because of what we looked like, but because of who we were.

If Junior Village taught me anything, it was that we're more alike than we think. Beneath the labels, the differences, and the walls we build, a shared humanity connects us all.

Hope would surface occasionally when my mother was allowed to visit. I held on to the dream that maybe this time, she would take me home. I clung to her during those visits, and when she left, the tears would return, soaking my pillow at night as I cried myself to sleep.

One day, a kind and beautiful young blonde lady came to visit me at Junior Village. To my 8-year-old self, she seemed like an angel. She asked if I wanted to visit my mother, and I excitedly said yes, overwhelmed with joy. We got in her car, and along the way, we stopped for ice cream sundaes. I never knew her name, but she was the most compassionate and picturesque woman I had ever seen. I still remember her bobbed hair, flipped at the ends, resting on her shoulders, and her floral fragrance. Though young, I was completely smitten with her kindness and beauty.

We arrived at what appeared to be a courthouse. After going through a few rooms, I saw my mother sitting behind a desk, separated from me by a glass partition—just like in the old movies where prisoners speak to visitors through a phone. I don't recall much of the conversation, but my mother reassured me she would come to get me soon, and I could count on it. After that, things became a blur. I wasn't at Junior Village for much longer than a year, and soon enough, I was reunited with my mother. It turns out she had written to her mother, my grandmother, in Mountain Home, Arkansas, asking if she could take me in until my mother sorted things out in DC. And just like that—I had a grandma!

Junior Village tested my limits but also taught me about shared humanity. Despite the loneliness and loss, I found fragments of strength in unexpected places—lessons that would become the bedrock of my survival.

Before I left for Arkansas, my mother found an apartment in Georgetown, a remarkable feat considering our financial situation. I had no idea where the money came from, but Georgetown was a significant upgrade from the dingy basement apartments we were used to.

It was early fall 1965, and I was starting fourth grade. One cool morning, my mother held my wrist so tightly that I thought it would break as we walked through the predominately Black neighborhoods of DC. As we hustled through the streets, I could smell freshly baked bread filling the air as we passed the Holmes Modern Bakery, housed in a gritty three-story building. That heavenly aroma became ingrained in my soul, sparking a lifelong love for freshly baked bread.

School was rough, as I anticipated it would be. Junior Village had given me some street smarts, so I learned how to navigate this new school called Seton. Most of the students, if not all, were Black, and I was the lone white kid again! I also knew enough to keep some extra milk money handy to avoid trouble with the bullies. The school year seemed to drag on, and the dread of getting into skirmishes daily was taxing me. Little by little, I made a few friends. I recall two brothers whose parents were very kind to us and would walk us through some of the tougher areas until we were close to the bus stop, where we caught the bus to Georgetown.

CHAPTER 3

Ozark Bound on a Hound

Then, one summer day, my grandmother's letter arrived, and soon after that, we were on "a hound a Greyhound bus that is to Arkansas." After several transfers, we arrived in Mountain Home, and there she was—a grandmother figure straight out of a Norman Rockwell painting.

I'll never forget her greeting: "Is this Carl? Hello, sweetheart; I'm so happy to meet you." I melted into her arms, and my mother received her share of hugs too. My grandfather was there, stoic but friendly enough. Our short time with them was special—this was the first time I had ever lived in a real house. It was a modest farmhouse, and they even had a car! They farmed and bartered with neighbors who lived miles apart, a far cry from the cramped city life of DC. I was in complete culture shock. My "Granny," as I called her, was a deeply spiritual woman. She regularly read her Bible and would talk to me about Jesus, sheep, and goats.

In Arkansas, I caught a glimpse of what life could be—stability, warmth, and the kind of family I'd only dreamed about. It wasn't flashy, just real. Granny's faith was like a quiet, steady heartbeat, always there, nudging me toward something bigger than myself. It planted a seed, though the roots wouldn't take hold for years.

Sundays were for church. A tiny white church set against a grassy field, straight out of a Coen Brothers movie like *O Brother, Where Art Thou*. Inside, it was mostly retirees, and I was the lone kid, bored stiff, secretly wishing for friends my age. Everyone called each other "Brother" or "Sister," a strange little ritual that felt both odd and oddly comforting.

Still, at night, I'd tuck my small, pocket-sized Bible under my pillow. It wasn't just a book—it was my lifeline, a gift from God that I believed had carried me out of my old life and into this new one.

My grandfather taught me how to shoot his rifle and shotgun. They bought me a Daisy BB gun, and I practiced shooting bottles. I would roam the nearby woods, shooting at trees and squirrels. Don't get too alarmed about the squirrels. The little BB gun did not affect them, and they just taunted me. When summer ended, my grandmother enrolled me in school in the fourth grade. I told my grandmother I had already finished fourth grade! She replied, "It won't hurt you to do it again." The school bus picked me up right in front of my grandparent's home, just like in *Forrest Gump*. I must have felt like Forrest having to repeat the fourth grade.

Now my mother had two sisters, Mary and Kathy. Mary and her husband, Andy, lived nearby in a fancy mountain home with a breathtaking view of Norfolk Lake. My Aunt Kathy and her husband, Paul, were from Houston and came up to visit. They were impeccably dressed and very warm toward me. I immediately felt a deep affection for Aunt Kathy and Uncle Paul, and the feeling was mutual. They discussed with my grandmother the possibility of me living with them in Houston, believing it would be better for me to be around children my age. They had a daughter, a few years older than me, who they thought could be like a big sister.

As much as I loved my granny, I jumped at the chance to live with them and experience something new. So, after a brief few weeks in the fourth grade in Mountain Home, Arkansas, I was again off to Houston via a Greyhound.

My aunt met me at the bus station, and with my little suitcase, we were off in her Chevy Caprice convertible. They had a beautiful home, complete with a swimming pool and two snooty French poodles. I had never experienced what was, to me, such a luxury. They enrolled me in Montgomery Elementary School in the fourth grade. I tried for fifth, but my granny told them to put me fourth. My uncle worked at a large Chevrolet dealership, and it seemed that he always drove a brand-new car. Their daughter, my cousin, was a pretty, outgoing blonde. She was an avid surfer and often took me with her to Galveston Island, where she and her friends would surf. I was in hog heaven. Meanwhile, my mother was still in DC, and I heard she was improving. My grandfather had managed to secure her widow's social security benefits from my deceased father, which were retroactive, giving her some financial relief.

Of course, nothing is ever perfect. My aunt and uncle both worked, and after they got home, my uncle often made a pitcher of martinis, which would lead to some verbal fireworks— sometimes even physical altercations. One night, things got so bad that my aunt shouted at me to call the police. "I don't know the number," I replied. My cousin and I still laugh about that now, but at the time, it was frightening.

The fourth grade in Houston differed from that in DC and Arkansas. It was much more difficult, and all that moving set me back as I was only good at reading. Thanks to comic books, I read at a higher level than my fellow students. However, the other subjects suffered, and I was on track to repeat the fourth grade again! Talk about feeling like Forrest Gump!

Eventually, my mother visited us in Houston—with a baby! She seemed more stable and sober-minded, though she didn't mention a husband. Well, I guess a lot can change in a year. She asked if I wanted to move to Florida with her. The idea of beaches and palm trees sounded too adventurous to pass up, and I felt compassion for my mother. So, we set off on a train bound for Jacksonville Beach, Florida. True to form, my mother didn't have a clue where we'd live; it felt like she had thrown a dart at a map and decided to follow wherever it landed.

CHAPTER 4

Corndogs and the Boardwalk

We moved to Jacksonville Beach, Florida, in the summer of 1967. My mother rented a one-room apartment with two beds and a bathroom off Third Street. I had this pit in my stomach and immediately felt homesick for Houston. In Houston, we had a lovely home, flawlessly decorated, and a pool. Aunt Kathy was meticulous in her home and a real foodie. My mother was quite the opposite. She was content with a roof over her head and a loaf of wonder bread. From here on out, I will refer to my mother as Marge. I had no contempt for her; I just had to find some humor in this whole ordeal. Marge was highly intelligent in a quirky sort of way, and her favorite book was the dictionary! She read every encyclopedia she could get her hands on. After a few days in our new surroundings, I made my way toward the beach and found the boardwalk. It reminded me of a small Coney Island that you would see on television with amusement rides, bumper cars, and a carny culture of local riffraff who played pinball and bummed cigarettes from passers-by. And then, there they were, the 12 to 14-year-old cigarette-smoking vagabonds, hanging out at the arcades and looking for mischief. I was the conscientious objector watching the local hooligans rack up the scores on those pinball machines and bumming more smokes and spare change to play arcade games. Marge gave me five bucks one day, and instantly, I had friends! Yes, riffraff, but companions nonetheless who showed me the ropes of boardwalk culture. My first dining experience at the boardwalk was at Goody's Corn Dogs. I never had a corn dog, and it was pretty tasty. This became my new name to identify things or certain behaviors, like "Stop acting like a corn dog" or "You're such a corn dog!"

When the five bucks ran out, so did the little leaches who I was hanging out with. They split to see where else they could find a host or buck up with some of the local "ride jocks" who were older and worldly-wiser and would sometimes give a free ride on the tilt-a-whirl.

No surprise when I got back to our no AC, stuffy little apartment, Marge demanded, "We're broke! Go ask your aunt to send us some money." Marge asked as if my aunt owed us a favor! I found a phone booth at the boardwalk and dropped in three valuable quarters for a long-distance call to Houston. When I heard my aunt's voice, I began to bawl like a baby.

In between sobs, I said, "Nothing has changed, and we are worse off than before."

Now, my aunt was a successful business lady, and she, rather matter-of-fact, said to me, "Carl, listen to me," her voice firm but not unkind. "Life isn't fair. You'll cry a lot less once you accept that. Now stop bawling and show the world what you're made of. I will send you some money this time, but I can't have you call me whenever you're broke. You must figure this out!"

Her words stung but stuck with me like a scar that reminded me of my strength.

Well, that was that! I suddenly felt as if I was on my own; yes, I was where the buck stopped, so to speak. I picked up a little job selling the *Beaches Leader* at the post office, which gave me a little pocket change. We eventually moved into a bigger place off First Street in the north sector of Jacksonville Beach.

Life on the boardwalk was an escape—a chance to reinvent myself amid the surf and the noise. Yet, deep down, I felt the pull of something more, a whisper that there was meaning beyond the waves and arcade lights.

It was Labor Day weekend, and school was about to start. I had to, yes, repeat the fourth grade again and was assigned to Mrs. Jacobson's fourth-grade class. I was becoming a master of the fourth grade and the oldest kid in the class. I felt like a dummy! Mrs. Jacobson was stern; she had cat-woman-style glasses with a chain attached to them. She did not put up with any Tom Foolery.

I would ride the city bus to school, which stopped right in front of my house. It took all the local fourth-grade kids to the San Pablo fourth-grade annex in South Jax Beach. I met all the local kids from Neptune Beach and Jax Beach. I thought riding the city bus sure beat riding in the yellow school bus.

I will say this about Mrs. Jacobson: she was the best teacher I ever had. She seemed to take a personal interest in me, and for the first time in my little life, I felt I could excel in school. Her belief in me was a quiet encouragement, and I began to see glimmers of a future beyond the struggles of the present.

I learned music, how baseball is played, and how to slide to home base from her. She was a rockstar fourth-grade teacher—tricky to find these days. I didn't fully understand it then, but she had sown the seeds of faith, resilience, and self-reliance.

Marge continued to struggle with her mental demons, and I found more odd jobs and another newspaper gig, which allowed me to have a route delivering the *Jacksonville Journal* from my bike. our social security benefits came in on the third of the month; I made money from the paper route, and Marge got a new job as a housekeeper at the new Holiday Inn. This all helped to ease some of our money issues. And the location was excellent. One day, Marge told some of the local riffraff, whom I would refer to as squawks in the neighborhood, that "Carl Garrett is a straight-A student and was not going to end up like trash dogs like you!" That was my mother's favorite word to describe the local riffraff.

They laughed their heads off! "Are you trying to get me killed?" I said to Marge. Fortunately, for my sake, they all thought that it was amusing. But that hit a chord in my gut, making me think, *Is this possible?* Soon after, I buckled down with my schoolwork, and thanks to Mrs. Jacobson's firm but loving way, I made a school patrol boy in the sixth grade with a uniform and badge. I became proficient in marching drills and was learning leadership skills.

On a hot summer day, I was scurrying across Third Street from the local grocery store wearing a pair of Bermuda shorts, no shirt, and sucking on an orange popsicle. I heard a man yelling at me from his third-floor apartment window off Third Street and Sixteenth Avenue North. He said, "Hey, kid, do you want a surfboard?"

Since moving to Florida, I had always dreamed of owning a surfboard, and I had been good at riding waves on rafts since my boardwalk days. I thought this was an opportunity of a lifetime, but *what's the catch?* "How much?" I replied.

Then he yelled, "I didn't say I was selling it! I said, 'Do you want it?'"

A bit stunned, I said meekly, "Yes, please!"

"Then come on up and get it," he said sternly.

Like a beach rat, I bolted up the stairs, a sticky mess of melted orange popsicle juice on my skinny little frame. A big, burly guy with a bandanna tied around his head, wearing an army jacket cut off from the shoulders that gave him the latest ex-military attire, greeted me. From the sound of Jimmy Hendrix blaring down the concrete stairway and lots of smoke, he was undoubtedly celebrating being home from Vietnam. And there he presented the biggest surfboard I have ever seen.

The guy said he got it in Hawaii and that it was shaped and custom-made by some famous Hawaiian dude. "All you have to do is get it down all those stairs," he said mockingly. I thanked the ex-soldier and cautiously maneuvered the hulking piece of craftmanship down the three flights of concrete stairs. Then I placed the water beast on my head and walked home, stopping to rest my aching head and arms on the way.

CHAPTER 5

Dogtown and The Holiday Inn

As I grew older, surfing became my sanctuary. Jacksonville Beach, with its rolling waves and golden sands, transformed from a mere backdrop into a stage where I could express freedom and find solace. The surf culture swept me up completely, and before long, I was spending more time at the beach than anywhere else. The boardwalk had been an introduction, but the surf was where I truly felt at home. I made new friends who shared my love of the waves. We spent endless hours reveling in the simple joy of the ocean. But along with this newfound camaraderie came a creeping rebellion. I began smoking pot, skipping school, and drifting toward a lifestyle of carefree indulgence. It was easy to lose sight of responsibility when the beach offered an escape from all that weighed me down.

The neighborhood kids around me were dropping out of school. However, something in me kept me in school only because I knew what it was like to be homeless and witnessed that way of life firsthand in Washington, DC. I told myself I would not be a bum! My aunt and mother always told me I would be successful and . . . *I was a Greek god.* Oh, brother!

The end of my junior high school years was formidable for me. Our junior high was a classic three-story Acme brick building built in the 1930s. I remember on one cool, rainy fall day, I sat at my desk gazing out those large Gothic windows that were wedged open for air circulation. I could hear and smell the fall rain gently tap on the window. As I looked outside, I noticed a familiar kid wearing a long trench coat and holding a large, tattered Bible under his arm cross the campus to the school's main entrance. Some Black kids were sitting behind me laughing and cutting up when one noticed the same fellow. He said in a loud, excited tone, "Hey, there's Doug." Someone asked if he was the kid's friend. "Man, what's wrong with you? Doug is everybody's friend," he replied. Now, I thought that was a high compliment to pay.

Later that evening, I was hitchhiking on First Street in Neptune Beach, heading south to Jax Beach. It was one of those crisp fall evenings with a slight warm breeze coming from the south. The harvest moon was full and bright and lit up the ocean like one of those perfect nights in a sleepy beach town. As I was hitching a ride, I noticed Doug, with his trench coat, long blond hair, and big Bible under his arm, thumbing a ride a few blocks ahead of me.

My initial thought was that he would get a ride before me. However, he noticed me and motioned that he was coming my way. He called out my name and suggested we hitch a ride together. It sounded okay to me. We chatted about school, and he asked how my mom and sister were doing. At about that time, a pickup truck pulled over to give us a lift. Some older surfer types, not saying a word, motioned for us to get in the back of the truck. We sat in the truck bed, and Doug started to talk. I thought, *Here it comes. He is going to talk about Jesus.* Sure enough, he asked, "Do you know Jesus?" Back then, it was acceptable to discuss Jesus as everyone supposedly was sort of a believer. After all, we revolted against the Beatles for claiming they were more popular than He was.

Jesus was just a familiar name, like something you'd hear in a Doobie Brothers song—"Jesus is just all right with me"—nothing more, nothing less. But then Doug shared something from the Bible that I'd never heard before: a passage about having the power to tread on snakes and scorpions, and over all the power of the enemy, and that nothing could harm you. He also mentioned that the spirits are subject to us, but we should rejoice because our names are written in heaven. It struck me in a way I hadn't expected. I felt this excitement and curiosity well up inside me, and I wanted to know more.

Doug led me in a prayer of salvation, and that night, I believed and accepted Jesus as my Savior. The moment was electrifying; I felt like something took hold of me, as if I was burning from within. It's hard to explain, but when we got out of the truck, I don't know if my feet touched the ground. We said goodbye and went our separate ways, but that night, I lay in bed, still buzzing with joy and hope from that moment.

But not long after, the peer pressure got me, and I slipped back into my old ways—chasing selfish desires and vanity, getting tangled up trying to be a popular surfer kid, making no effort to accept that grace or understand the concept of being saved. I lacked in the faith department. Faith is like a fire. It'll keep burning as long as you feed it. Strangely enough, I was rescued and didn't know it. I was free from a perpetual state of sin but clueless about what my part was in all of it.

Living in Jacksonville Beach was starting to improve for me. The summer of 1972 marked a memorable time in my life. I made new friends who appeared to have higher standards than my prior ones. One summer afternoon, while waxing my surfboard, a Baptist preacher approached me and asked, "Do you know where you'll be if you die today?" I dismissively replied that I had no idea, didn't care, and wasn't interested. He simply nodded and moved on, gathering local kids for Vacation Bible School. My sister was among them, as he saw a need to guide the unsaved youth in our neighborhood. I never forgot that encounter; over time, I felt ashamed for acting rudely. Looking back, I see myself as a disrespectful punk who needed a serious attitude adjustment. In junior high, I definitely had more than my share of "the board of education applied to the seat of knowledge" from the dean, if you catch my drift.

Landing an actual job at fifteen felt like stepping into a new world. It wasn't glamorous, but it came with a paycheck, which made all the difference. I was hired as a dishwasher at the Holiday Inn in Jacksonville Beach, Florida—a place tolerant of a long-haired surfer kid like me. In those days, work for teenagers was scarce, especially during the bustling summer tourist season. I considered myself lucky.

The Holiday Inn wasn't just another job; it was a step up. I think the area needed a place like this, and somehow, it felt like the right place for me too. At $1.65 an hour, the going minimum wage, that steady paycheck meant freedom—which was priceless.

I'll never forget my first day. It was a hot, humid summer afternoon, and the hotel was packed with tourists. The kitchen buzzed with energy—a mix of sizzling pans, clanging dishes, and hurried voices. The chef gave me a long, skeptical look and muttered under his breath, "Another long-haired surfer kid." I knew he was thinking: *This kid won't last a week.*

But then he sent me to RG, a 16-year-old veteran of the dish pit who was full of hard-earned wisdom. He handed me my uniform—a stiff, white button-down shirt, an apron, and a paper hat that made me look like a soda jerk. "Guard this towel with your life," he said, handing me a clean kitchen towel like it was a badge of honor. "They ration these like gold."

RG took me through the chaotic kitchen, explaining the ropes. I followed him past racks of glasses stacked high, rows of stainless-steel shelves crammed with bus tubs overflowing with dishes, and the Hobart—the loud, steaming beast of a dishwashing machine that would become my nemesis. "Get mad at those dishes," RG said. "Go into attack mode. It's the only way to survive, or you'll feel like you've been sent straight to hell." I thought he was exaggerating—until the dinner rush hit.

The radio perched on top of the Hobart played AM hits from the summer of 1972—Chicago's "Saturday in the Park," Don McLean's "American Pie," Gilbert O'Sullivan's "Alone Again Naturally." Those melodies, mixed with the clatter of plates and the shouts of cooks, created a soundtrack for my new reality. Even now, those songs take me back to those days hanging out at the Holiday Inn.

That job taught me more than just how to scrub plates or stack glasses. It taught me to show up, work hard, and take pride in even the simplest tasks. It wasn't just a paycheck but the start of something bigger.

The Holiday Inn sat on the beach, and the surf there had a nice break. Taking out the garbage became my favorite part of the job. It allowed me to breathe in the salty air, check out the waves, and reconnect with my friends. My life revolved around the ocean and the Holiday Inn. Surfing and work—it was as good as it got.

Looking back, those were some of the best days of my life. The parties, the friends, and the endless waves were a chapter of freedom and growth, a time when life was full of promise and simple joys. It wasn't just about the Holiday Inn; it was about finding my place in a world that, for a little while, felt like paradise.

The father of one of my friends, Charlie, was a circuit judge in Jacksonville. "The Judge," as we called him, was a wise man who always made time for me and offered sound advice. Without a father figure growing up, I came to value my conversations with him. Now, surfers have a habit of giving each other nicknames or calling one another by their last name, so I became "Carlos," while my friends had names like Champ, Brown, Day, Green, Skeeter, Lips, Koke Spoon, and Bozo. Strange as they sound, each one was given with respect, believe it or not.

And I can't forget the beach girls. They were smart and full of life, and many went on to great success. They had their own names too—Fro, Rixen, Darky (for Angie, my first girlfriend, who loved her suntans), KJ, Flossy, and of course, Barbie. Those memories—the surf, the friendships, and those sunny, carefree days—shaped who I am in ways I'll always carry with me.

We lived in a small garage apartment nestled behind a cluster of other weathered apartments, their peeling paint giving them the tired, beach-town effect. It had a quietness but a quiet that came and went in waves. Most of the surrounding apartments were rented by navy personnel—sailors, or "squids," as we liked to call them.

When they were on leave, the neighborhood came alive, buzzing with parties that stretched late into the night. Music, boisterous laughter, and the shouting that only happens when sailors let loose filled the air. But when the sailors shipped out, gone on their six-month or year-long cruises, the neighborhood fell into a stillness. Those stretches of peace? Blissful.

I attended the local beach schools—San Pablo Elementary, Fletcher Junior High, and Fletcher Senior High. It was slow and steady, much like everything else in that small slice of Jacksonville Beach life. I kept my job at the Holiday Inn, starting as a dishwasher and working my way up to the bar and lounges as a steward or bar back. It wasn't glamorous, but it gave me skills I didn't even realize I was learning at the time—how to mix drinks, stock inventory, and keep the back of the house running smoothly.

Most of my time was spent stocking bar products for two of the hotel's main spots: the Vice Admiral Lounge on the first floor and the rooftop lounge upstairs. Back then, we had real lounge singers—the kind you only hear about now with voices that carried stories from the stage straight to the listener. In the Vice Admiral Lounge was Sandy Smith, sitting behind her electric organ, singing smooth jazz and crooning hits from the '50s and '60s. Upstairs in the rooftop lounge, One Fell Swoop, a six-piece band, filled the room with energy. It wasn't just music—it was the soundtrack to the early evening buzz of conversation, clinking glasses, and the soft hum of neon lights.

At 4:00 p.m. sharp, the local businessmen would trickle in for happy hour. They came for the camaraderie, the drinks, and, of course, the complimentary snacks. Swedish meatballs, little roasted cocktail weenies in a questionable BBQ sauce, and trays of crudités were standard fare. To them, it wasn't just food—it was ritual, a brief respite from the day's grind.

Looking back, it was a simple time, but it felt full. Every job, every shift, every voice in the lounge taught me something, even if I didn't realize it then. I learned to pay attention—to the rhythm of people's lives, to how fleeting moments become lasting memories, and to how even the most minor, unnoticed tasks can lay the foundation for something far greater.

I drifted through high school without much thought for the future. My world was the beach—surfing waves, chasing pretty girls, weekend parties, and hanging out with friends. Life was carefree, without structure or demands, and I did as I pleased. Music was our constant companion, shaping the days and soundtracking the nights. I had stacks of vinyl records—Led Zeppelin, Johnny Winter, all the greats—but back then, Lynyrd Skynyrd was just a local band, a group of rowdy guys making noise around Jacksonville.

At first, I didn't care for them. They seemed brash, rough around the edges—nothing special. But one morning, as I got ready for school, something changed. A song hit the radio, and the guitar riffs stopped me cold. They were powerful, the kind that grabs you by the collar and doesn't let you go. The DJ's voice broke in: "That was 'Free Bird' by Jacksonville's own Lynyrd Skynyrd." I stood there, stunned. *Wait, those guys made that?* From then on, I couldn't ignore them. That moment flipped my perception of the band forever.

Looking back now, I understand what people mean when they say history repeats itself, that there's nothing new under the sun. Alvin Lee from Ten Years After, one of my favorite bands, wrote, "I'd love to change the world, but I don't know what to do." That line stuck with me. *Who's supposed to change the world anyway? And what are they waiting for?*

At the time, the Vietnam War loomed over everything. The draft hung like a shadow, and the thought of being sent overseas wasn't something you could escape. Beyond that? I had no idea what came next. When the war ended in 1975, so did my immediate fear of being drafted. Relief washed over me, but it didn't answer the bigger question—*What do I do with my life?*

Those years were like a song—raw, uncertain, and alive. We all thought we had plenty of time to figure everything out. But life doesn't work that way. The clock never stops. Every moment builds into the next, even when you're not paying attention. I didn't think about responsibility back then. I didn't worry about purpose. I was just along for the ride. But now, looking back, I can see how those carefree days were part of a larger story—one God was already writing. Even when I couldn't see it, He was shaping something. I didn't know it then, but He was there, weaving purpose into everything.

After graduating from high school in 1976, I reconnected with family in Houston. I spent the summer working odd jobs at my uncle's car dealership to save money for my first semester at Florida Junior College, which we jokingly called Fletcher Jr. College after the junior high and high school we had attended. Between painting parking curbs and fixing fences, I also experienced Houston nightlife, visiting my cousin who worked as a bartender at Uncle Sam's Disco. I enjoyed the height of the disco era, sipping hurricane cocktails and bourbon & Coke to the sounds of the Bee Gees, Donna Summer, and Barry White, with a nod to Willie Nelson and Waylon Jennings.

CHAPTER 6

Life After the Beach

After that summer, I started college, aiming high with pre-med and medical laboratory technology. It sounded important, even noble. But by midsemester, I was drowning under a 17-hour course load, barely keeping my head above water. To make ends meet, I took a part-time job at Jax Liquors in Atlantic Beach, where I quickly became an unofficial expert on every kind of alcohol we sold. The highlight of the job was running the drive-through—a concept that felt ahead of its time, like Chick-fil-A but handing over cases of beer and bottles of spirits.

As my studies faltered, my social life found a new center: Pete's Bar in Neptune Beach. House parties were still around, but I was shifting into a different rhythm, a slightly older, though not necessarily wiser, chapter of life. Pete's Bar was my new go-to. It was a cramped local dive, reeking of stale beer and cigarette smoke, always loud enough to make conversation a shouting match. I remember muttering to myself once, *If you're not careful, you're going to end up a beach bum hanging out at Pete's.*

The crowd at Pete's was a mix of rowdy old surfers, troublemakers, and, of course, beach girls—one of the main reasons I kept going back. Fights were a nightly spectacle, usually breaking out over someone cutting in on a pool game.

Looking back, I couldn't help but wonder if the Jax Beaches carried a strange, dark undercurrent. Drunkenness, drug use, and immorality seemed to hang in the air like a fog, seeping into everything. At the time, I didn't resist it—I was part of it, a willing participant in the chaos.

Meanwhile, my family in Houston stayed connected, checking in regularly. One day, after I vented to my aunt about the pressures of school and my struggle to find decent work, she cut straight to the point: "Come back to Houston," she said sharply. "You can enroll at the University of Houston and work two jobs like the rest of us." The idea of making more money was tempting, and before long, I packed up my things and headed for Texas.

But I didn't dive back into school right away. Instead, I found my way into the restaurant industry—a world that seemed to click with me immediately. It felt natural, like I'd stumbled into something I was meant to do. Houston's thriving restaurant scene was magnetic, and I couldn't resist. I started as a bartender and server, cutting my teeth at legendary spots like Daddy's Money and Delmonico's in the Galleria Plaza Hotel. The fast pace, the rhythm of service, and the energy of the industry pulled me in. For a while, it felt like enough, like I'd found my stride.

Eventually, I stepped away from the restaurant world and landed a solid job as a wireline operator at Schlumberger. A regular customer from the bar vouched for me, and just like that, I was in. The pay was good, and the work offered stability, but the hours were brutal. Life started moving faster than I could keep up. Somewhere in that whirlwind, I got married and joined the Jehovah's Witnesses (JW), believing they had the answers I sought. It felt right at the time—a steady path forward. I started a family and tried to settle into this version of life.

Then the oil crash hit. The pay cut that followed knocked me off balance. Suddenly, the stable life I'd been building wasn't so stable anymore. That's when I returned to what I knew best: the restaurant business.

Back in the fold, I worked for chains like TGI Fridays, Houston's, and Houlihan's. It was the heyday of the "happy hour wars"—bars packed wall to wall every night and brunch lines that snaked around the block. Each restaurant had its own personality. Some ran on a "work hard, play hard" mentality; others demanded precision and a relentless drive for perfection.

Houlihan's stood out most, thanks to Ron Barkley, a sharp, no-nonsense leader who practically built the brand from the ground up. Ron wasn't just a boss—he was a teacher. He drilled into me the art and science of restaurant management, pushing me to see beyond the day-to-day grind. "Corporate restaurants aren't for entrepreneurs," he said one day. "If you want to do things your way, you'll have to step out on your own."

The idea of stepping out felt impossible. I knew I didn't fit the corporate mold, but the thought of leaving the safety of it terrified me. Then, at a Brinker International conference, the reality of my career smacked me square in the face. During an awards ceremony, a fellow general manager leaned over and quietly said, "Carl, there are no retirement plans or gold watches in this business." I knew he was right. It was the confirmation of a truth I'd been trying to ignore: I was stuck—managing restaurants with no real future, no clear path forward, and no endgame in sight.

By 1996, I had hit my breaking point. My marriage was crumbling, the religion I'd turned to for answers was not ringing that truth with me, and my career felt like a treadmill, taking me nowhere. I couldn't shake the feeling that I was running in circles. For years, I'd dreamed of restaurant concepts and sketched out menus, but this time, something shifted. I knew I couldn't keep dreaming—I had to start doing. The decision wasn't easy. Leaving the safety of structure and familiarity felt like jumping off a cliff. Friends and family warned me: "Stick to the steady job," they said. "You're too much of a dreamer." But for the first time, I wasn't looking for practical advice—I was looking for a chance.

And I was ready to take it.

*****

That year, I moved to Seattle to help a local restaurant group launch a new concept. It was supposed to be a fresh start, a chance to prove what I could do. But instead of embracing my ideas, the head of the concept shot me down at every turn. He rejected everything I suggested, brushing me off like I didn't belong. His dismissal crushed me. I was 40 years old, standing in the wreckage of what I thought might finally be my big break.

By 1997, I was still in Seattle, managing a busy southwestern-style restaurant. I hoped a multi-unit management opportunity would open if I worked hard enough. Maybe this could be my moment. But deep down, the entrepreneurial itch wouldn't go away. I kept shoving it down, telling myself, *Buckle down. Don't be stupid. If you don't stick with this, you'll end up a failure—or worse, a bum.*

Friends, family, and even colleagues agreed: I'd never own my own business. "It's out of your reach," they said. "Just accept it. Keep your job and move on." I tried to listen, but something inside me kept saying otherwise.

Then one evening, everything changed. One of my waiters mentioned an upscale Asian restaurant in Belltown where he worked part-time. The owner, he said, wanted to meet me. "I've been telling him you're the perfect person to run the place," the waiter explained. For the first time in a long while, hope flickered again. So, I left my stable, high-volume southwestern restaurant in an A+ location with great pay and benefits for a low-volume, poorly located spot with lousy parking and a pay cut, all to take a chance on creating the next big concept. Who knows, maybe I'd see my name in *Restaurant News* and win an award for launching the next hot trend!

I met with the owner, who seemed like a nice guy, and we hashed out a vague agreement for me to have a stake in the business. It didn't take long for me to realize that the owner had multiple partners, was behind on bills and taxes, and even had a construction lien on the building—who knows what else! But being naive and eager to become a legitimate entrepreneur, I dove in, determined to turn this struggling restaurant around and transform it into a thriving concept. After a few months, however, the World Trade

Organization (WTO) protests hit and shut down the area, putting the final nail in the coffin for this little venture.

One evening in late April, the owner and I sat down for a final meal, accompanied by a glass of cabernet, and reflected on where things went wrong. He looked at me and said, "Carl, look around—you did it!"

"Did what?" I asked, confused.

"Look at the business! The bar is packed with Gen Xers, the restaurant has a waitlist, and the staff seems happy!"

I felt a moment of satisfaction, but reality quickly set in. *This was our last night of business, and I'm crying out loud! As they say, we were a day late and a dollar short.* The owner pointed out that we were simply undercapitalized, and that had taken its toll. *How did I not see that from the beginning? Why was I such a fool? What was my problem?* Now I was flat broke—or more like in the negative! I berated myself further: *What an idiot! What was I supposed to do now?*

I went home to my tiny apartment in Queen Anne, with a view of the Space Needle, much like Frazer Crane's. It felt like I was stuck in the Twilight Zone. I needed a break—some kind of escape from this mess. At that point, the only thing left to do was pray. I gave it my best shot and simply asked God for a way out. "I know you're there," I said. "I've made a huge mess of everything—relationships, finances, and business. I've taken the wrong path!" Yes, made the wrong choice again!

I wasn't religious then, not a churchgoer or a Christian by any means. I felt like a fish out of water regarding church matters.

But despite my foolishness, I felt a connection to God. I didn't know if He could even hear me or if He cared at all. But I prayed anyway because it was my last option. You could say I hit rock bottom and needed an emergency U-turn. I'm not sure what happened to that little pocket Bible companion I had as a kid, but I sure could have used it under my pillow that night.

Well, I actually got an answer to my prayer. A few days later, a buddy of mine in Houston, an Italian guy, called to ask if I needed a job. Fighting back tears and my stubborn pride, I told him I was "entertaining some offers."

"Yeah, right," he said. "Well, when you're done playing around in Seattle, there's a GM (General Manager) position in Houston. The pay is good, and it's a solid company. They offered me the job, but I turned it down, suggesting someone else like you take it."

Well, I jumped at the chance and got hired. Just like that, I left Seattle's gloominess and returned to Houston's familiar territory. I thanked my friend but didn't acknowledge God who was really pulling the strings behind the scenes. You might say I was foolish in my ungratefulness.

It was the year 2000, and we all survived Y2K. I was running an Italian restaurant in the West University area of Houston. Having been thrown a lifeline by the Almighty Himself, I was still blind to the effect of that gracious gift of hope and another chance. That little period of attempting to operate my own place in Seattle devastated me financially. The decent salary I received wasn't enough to compensate for all my losses, and once again, the future looked grim.

The divorce situation also had a huge financial impact, and I spent most of my time at the restaurant as I had very little money for anything else. Then, one evening, while working at the front desk, I met a lovely lady from South Africa. She was arranging a farewell party for a friend and had a large group to celebrate. We made small talk and exchanged business cards. I was reluctant to follow up with her as I was empty in spirit and finances. Then, a few months later, I came across her card while cleaning out my wallet. I thought, *If I called her, she probably wouldn't remember me. But here goes, let's find out.* Well, she recalled our conversation, and we made a dinner date. As we continued to date, she wanted to attend church and suggested I accompany her.

Now, My ex-spouse was a Jehovah's Witness, and I joined the religion with her many years ago. Truth be told, I was never more than a seat-warmer in the Kingdom Hall—a passive observer who went through the motions without much involvement. But one thing was drilled into me: stepping into any church outside the JW faith would bring serious spiritual consequences, or so they said.

This remarkable lady I met at the restaurant was on her own faith journey. She wanted to visit different churches, and for reasons I couldn't quite explain, I decided to join her. Having already been shown the "left foot of fellowship" from the JW organization, I figured I didn't have much to lose. I braced myself for judgment, lightning bolts, or maybe the ceiling collapsing on my head. But as we walked into those churches, one after another, none of those things happened. Instead, I felt something unexpected: curiosity.

Let me say a word about folks in the JW faith. At the heart of it, they're just like the rest of us—searching for truth, meaning, and the deeper purpose of life. While I've wrestled with their doctrine and found it hard to reconcile, I won't tear them down. That's not my place. I'll leave the judging to God. I believe that if you genuinely want the truth, God will ensure it finds you. He's faithful that way, always reaching out, always opening doors for those willing to seek Him.

We explored several churches around Houston, trying to find the right place. My friend was searching for something specific, though she couldn't quite put it into words. On the other hand, I realized I wouldn't have known a "perfect fit," even if it came with neon signs pointing the way. But through the process, I started to see that the search itself was doing something to me. It was working on my faith and giving me courage. I realized God was meeting me in the act of seeking, showing me that He wasn't confined to a building or a denomination. Sometimes, the hardest step is the first one out of fear, or as the Chinese proverb states, the journey of a thousand miles begins with a step, and that step leads to freedom.

One day, she turned to me and said, "Let's go to Lakewood Church."

I wasn't exactly thrilled. "Lakewood?" I said with a raised eyebrow. "All those guys want is your money! I've seen that preacher on TV, going on about the 'oasis of love.'" I laughed to myself and muttered, "Yeah, the oasis of love that fleeces you for every dime you've got." I went on, lumping Lakewood's preacher in with every scandal and other TV preacher I'd ever heard about. "They're all the same—scammers and con men."

She gave me a look that said *you're talking nonsense, and you know it.*

"All right," I finally said. "If you think it's a good idea, let's go."

It took me a while to get used to the place. Lakewood was big and loud, not at all what I pictured church to be, but I liked the preacher, Joel. It was the summer of 2001, and he'd just taken over from his dad, John Osteen, who had passed away the year before. Joel didn't preach like anyone I'd heard before. His message wasn't heavy-handed or full of fire and brimstone. It was positive, uplifting even. He seemed genuine, not the flashy kind I was expecting.

Still, I was cautious. When the offering bucket came my way, I'd pass it along, pretending to put something in. The truth was, I couldn't spare a dollar, and honestly, I didn't believe in giving money to a church. *What do they even do with it?* I thought. *Probably spend it on who knows what.*

But week by week, something shifted. It wasn't the flashy promises or the big production that drew me in. It was the simplicity of the message—hope, faith, and trusting God for a better future. It was a reminder that maybe, just maybe, my assumptions about church and God weren't the whole story.

CHAPTER 7

Divine Intervention

By the time a month had passed, church had started to feel different—almost attractive. I found myself looking forward to Sunday mornings. I figured it was better to be mocked as a "little Christian" than to keep living as a bent man, stuck on my own skewed terms. It was clear that my way wasn't working. Even if I made it to a hundred years old, what then? What did I have to lose?

One Sunday, Joel started talking about finances, and I braced myself. *Here we go, the money talk.* But it wasn't what I expected. We were sitting in the nosebleed seats at Lakewood's old location in east Houston long before they moved to the massive arena they call home now. Joel's face appeared on the screen of my mind with eyes shut tight, and then, with a tone that almost cut through the air, he declared, "Satan, get your hands off our finances!"

The words hit me like a jolt of lightning. Something inside me jumped before I even realized what was happening. Without thinking, I shouted, "Yeah!" It was instinctive, not calculated, and for a second, I looked around, expecting people to stare.

But no one did. They were just as locked in, their hands raised, eyes closed, shouting their own amens and agreements. The idea that the devil could be stealing from me—stealing opportunities, stealing provision—was a whole new concept. And then Joel said something else: "Give us a year of your life, and it will change for the better." That challenge stuck with me. My life was already at rock bottom. What did I have to lose? So, I decided to invest myself fully, to take that U-turn and become a regular at Lakewood Church.

As I continued to attend, something in me shifted, like an engine slowly engaging first gear. I started dropping small amounts of money—whatever I could spare—into the offering bucket. "All right, God," I'd mutter, "I'm trusting You with this." I had always been skeptical of preachers who promised jets and mansions, but this felt different. If there was wisdom in this about getting out of debt or turning things around, I wanted to learn. I started to understand that God doesn't want us stuck in an endless struggle. The message began to sink in: *To whom much is given, much will be required.*

I joined a men's group that met on Saturday mornings. It wasn't anything grand or flashy, but little by little, my faith began to grow. My financial troubles didn't vanish overnight—I was still behind on bills, and my lawyer never failed to remind me of how much I owed him. His timing, of course, was always impeccable. It felt like some financial adversary was always waiting to remind me of my struggles. At times, I wondered, *Is this just my lot in life?*

One day, I heard a preacher claim that everything in our lives is predestined. It left me pondering a deeper question: *If life is already predestined, then what's the point of praying?* A simple yet profound truth came to light as I wrestled with this thought. God is not a God of contradiction or deceit—He is Truth itself. And because He is truth, I can confidently say this: Fight for the life you've been given. Pray boldly. Ask without hesitation. Believe in His best for you. To do otherwise—to sit back and accept suffering as "God's plan"—isn't faith; it's fatalism. Scripture makes it clear: *Knock. Seek. Ask.* These aren't suggestions; they're commands (see Matthew 7:7).

Consider Sarah in Genesis Chapter 18, who laughed at the thought of bearing a child in her old age. She didn't laugh out loud—only in her heart. Yet God heard her doubt and called her out, saying, "Why did you laugh?" Startled, she denied it, but the Lord replied firmly, "Yes, you did laugh." In that moment, Sarah must have realized that if the Lord could hear the unspoken doubts of her heart, He could certainly make the impossible possible. And He did. Her doubt was replaced by faith—a faith that ushered in a miracle.

Then came September 11, 2001—a day when the world seemed to stand still. I was in Maui for a manager's conference when the news broke. Planes had struck the towers, and chaos rippled across the nation. Even on that isolated island, the weight of the tragedy was palpable. It felt surreal to be in a place so beautiful while the rest of the world unraveled. Amid the uncertainty, my old friend Bill called and mentioned that Chuck, another mutual friend, was also in Maui. Not long after, Chuck showed up, surfboard in hand and a grin that didn't match the day's heaviness. "Got an extra board in the truck," he said casually. "Let's hit the water."

So, we did. Out there, beyond the noise and chaos, the ocean had a way of quieting everything. The waves didn't care about tragedy or uncertainty; they rolled in steady and constant, as if to whisper, *This, too, shall pass.* The salt spray was refreshing, and the rhythm of paddling calmed the storm inside me. It didn't erase the weight of what was happening onshore, but it offered something precious—perspective.

As I sat on my board, drifting with the rhythm of the waves, questions swirled in my mind. *How would I get back to Houston? Could I rebuild—financially, emotionally, spiritually?* And deeper still, *was it time to take a leap of faith into marriage again?* The answers weren't clear, but the ocean reminded me that life keeps moving forward. Sometimes, in the middle of a storm, you're handed a surfboard instead of a life ring. And in the slightest, most unexpected moments, clarity begins to emerge.

I think back to the pocket-sized Bible I clung to as a frightened little boy, alone in the dark. I didn't understand much of it then, but I knew it mattered. I prayed. And somehow, in ways I couldn't explain, I was led to safety—to the loving arms of my grandparents. Faith is like the wind. You can't see it, but you feel its effects. Or like gravity—it's invisible, but it pulls everything into place. God created not just what is visible but what is invisible as well. There's always more happening than meets the eye. He gave us His Word, not just as a book, but as a guide—a compass for navigating both realms and, most importantly, for hearing from Him directly. Prayer fueled by faith is the spark that sets everything in motion. It's what makes miracles happen.

*****

When I returned to work, I knew something had to change. I wasn't just running on empty financially—I was drained as a man. There's a metaphor about the potter and the clay. I, the clay, had missed the whole point of what the potter was shaping. I saw broken fragments; He saw potential. And He wasn't done with me yet. I assure you, He's not done with you either. So, there's no point in squawking about it.

Even when I didn't feel like it, I prayed. Constantly. I felt like a little pest; I kept asking God for help. Not the kind of prayer you toss into the void and forget, but the kind that rises from a place of raw desperation—the kind where you mean every word. I wanted to be better. I wanted to be right. And though I didn't realize it then, the Potter was still at work.

One afternoon, I knelt in my small office, the hum of the restaurant around me, and bowed my head on the chair. "God," I said, "please help me." And that's when it happened. It wasn't a whisper or a nudge. It was a voice—sharp, clear, and impossible to ignore. It didn't speak from the room but from somewhere deep inside, where there's no hiding. The words hit me like a lightning bolt: **"STOP STEALING."**

There's a Hebrew word, *Shema*. It doesn't just mean to hear but to listen and respond. And that's precisely what this was for me—a *Shema* moment. The command was plain, unmistakable, and terrifying. I sat there, stunned. My thoughts unraveled in a rush, exposing every corner I'd cut, every selfish decision I'd justified. I remembered bartering restaurant gift certificates for personal gain and using company funds like they were mine. I had been dishonest, and now there was no pretending otherwise. God had called me out.

That moment shook me to the core. I was scared senseless. My heart raced, and I knew I couldn't brush this off or delay a response. This wasn't a suggestion but a line drawn in the sand. From that day on, if I found a single penny on the restaurant floor, it went into the cash drawer. No exceptions.

It wasn't just about the money; it was about trust between me and my employer, between me and myself, and between me and God. I realized that had given me stewardship over something that wasn't mine, and I had failed to honor that responsibility. But I wasn't going to fail again. Some serious changes needed to happen in my choices and how I conducted my life. I could tell God wanted a character change in me before any further assistance from Him. That moment taught me a lesson I'll never forget: faith is about action. It's not enough to hear—you must change. That's what it means to listen.

Now, despite all my drama, my soon-to-be wife accepted my proposal after much prayer. She must have seen something special in me because I wasn't seeing what she was. We got married at Lakewood Church at the end of March 2002. I was now a born-again believer and very aware that God was in my life to stay.

Six months later, in September 2002, an owner of a local restaurant approached me. He wanted to build a team and was in contact with my former kitchen manager, who was and still is a dear friend. My friend suggested I take the lead and restart his tired restaurant concept. He offered me significantly more money and even paid me cash for the little stock investment I had built in the restaurant I was leaving.

I still had a lot to learn, and God was training me and working on my character and pride. Because I had little moral character and a lot of pride, a few months at the church was not going to fix it. But God knew how.

I left the Italian restaurant to join this new venture. The restaurant I was taking over had been in the Houston area since the late 1980s and was known for its fajitas. The owner wanted a fresh start as the former concept was tired and needed a new life. Now, I was embarking on something similar to the Asian bistro in Seattle, but this time, I did a little homework. The owner was capitalized, and no creditors that I could tell were after him.

From the first couple of weeks of working with him, I could tell there would be some head-butting. I was given autonomy in developing the brand, writing the menu, and developing the recipes. We opened the restaurant with a new menu, staff, and a fresh start. We were on our way slowly but surely; however, the owner was a stubborn and impatient man. He felt the menu was too high-end for his clientele and scrubbed everything I did. This frustrated the staff, and most of them ended up leaving. The owner's son had to pick up the slack in the kitchen, and I did the same in the front. My kitchen manager was still hanging in there, as he and I quit our jobs to work in this antagonistic environment.

I could tell he wanted me out, as my salary was becoming a burden. I quit with a "today's notice" and left that day. I figured I'd get another job and move on. This turned out to be much more challenging than I realized. I was newly married and unemployed, which was not a good way to begin.

You can probably imagine the weight of it all—the strain it put on my new marriage, the toll it took on me personally. *Why wasn't I catching a break? I went to church. I read my Bible. I confessed Jesus as Lord. So, what gives?* There I was, back in the job market—older, struggling financially, and hoping for something to shift. But just because I'd found Christ didn't mean my circumstances magically changed. Faith doesn't work that way.

I was determined to land a good job with a solid company and a respectable salary. But door after door stayed closed. Hillstone, Cheesecake Factory, and other big-name restaurant groups weren't even giving me a second glance. I was sinking, slowly but surely, losing the sense of who I was.

Once, I was a successful restaurant operator. Now? I was nothing—or at least, that's how it felt. My identity had always been wrapped up in that title: *restaurateur*. Without it, I felt invisible, insignificant. I started hearing the lies in my head: *I'm too old. Washed up. A has-been.* Desperation led me to apply for jobs I'd never have considered before. Companies that, deep down, I knew weren't a fit. Even they could see something was off. I'll never forget the look on one manager's face when I applied to a low-end wing joint in one of the worst parts of Houston. His expression said it all: *Why is someone like you even here?*

I couldn't buy a job, no matter how hard I tried.

It was a full-blown identity crisis. I'd built my life around the idea that my value came from my profession—that my worth was tied to my title. But this ordeal forced me to face an uncomfortable truth: I am not my job. A career or a paycheck doesn't define my worth. I'm more than that. But letting go of that mindset was the hardest part. It felt like pulling apart the threads of who I thought I was and starting over from scratch.

Even amid this struggle, the Lord kept me busy. Doors didn't open, but interviews came. It was as if He was keeping me occupied, giving me small steps while I waited for the bigger picture to unfold. I chased opportunities in Miami, New Orleans, Dallas, and even Brownsville, Texas. Each time, I thought, *This is it. This will be the one.* But time and time again, nothing came to fruition. Every rejection chipped away at the man I thought I was, but something more profound was beginning to take root. I didn't realize it then, but God was teaching me to let go of the identity I'd built for myself and lean into the one He had planned for me.

I had never felt this type of worthlessness. In the past, I always knew I was in the driver's seat, confident, good at my profession, and in demand, but not then. Something was strangely different. I returned to prayer, but differently. I started fasting and praying. I would go to church four to five services a week. I volunteered at the church and attended every Saturday's men's group. Sometimes, there was a break at the men's group and no meetings. That was discouraging. I needed that group meeting and the interaction and spiritual upbuilding.

My wife and I would sometimes attend three church services on Sunday, two in the morning and one in the evening. We would go to Wednesday night Bible teaching. We attended a small home group—anything to keep us close to God and busy at the same time. We both prayed and fasted for a breakthrough. We even deposited our coins in the coin machine for cash. Over four months passed with no job and no income. My wife was a South African citizen and could not legally work in the US.

I contacted my former boss in Dallas, who once owned Canyon Café and Sam's Café. Back in the late '90s, he sold the businesses to another restaurant group and had done well for himself. He was investing in technology and other ventures those days, but his love for the restaurant industry hadn't faded. I pitched him my Florida-style restaurant concept, but he wasn't interested. Still, he invited me to Dallas to discuss ideas. We even talked about possibly buying back one of the restaurants I'd operated in Seattle. He said he'd make me a sweat equity partner if that happened. The idea was thrilling—a dream, really—but a long shot. The current owners didn't seem like the type to sell, at least not for the price my former boss would offer. And even if they did, getting the right lease terms was another hurdle.

That opportunity became the focus of my prayers. I begged God to open a door, to make a way for us to move to Seattle, and for me to have another chance at running that restaurant. This time, I vowed, things would be different. I'd care for it as if it were my own, report humbly to my boss, and do whatever it took to make it a success. I was ready to work a hundred hours a week if that's what it took.

But the bills didn't stop, and the checking account was draining fast. Desperation started setting in. One day, I even drove down to the Houston shipyards to see about cleaning out cargo containers. I figured it was hard, honest work—something to keep us afloat. But that idea hit a wall when I learned I'd need to join the union first. I came home empty-handed and deflated, with nothing good to report.

Back at home, I made a pot of coffee, settled onto the couch, and turned on the TV. Back then, Christian programming often filled our evenings. That night, I landed on *The 700 Club*. Terry Meeuwsen and Gordon Robertson were leading a prayer segment, sharing what they called words of knowledge— messages from God meant for viewers. Usually, it was for healing, which didn't feel like it applied to me. The whole thing reminded me of *Romper Room* from when I was a kid. If you're old enough, you'll remember—the woman with the magic mirror would pretend to see children's faces through it, calling out random names. As a kid, I sat glued to the screen, hoping she'd call my name. She never did.

That night, though, Ms. Meeuwsen wasn't just praying for the sick. She paused mid-prayer as if something had caught her attention and said, "I see a man sitting on a couch. Behind him is a vase with red flowers. You need a job. I want you to know that God is working things out for you. Don't despair."

I froze. Her words hit me like a thunderclap. A man on a couch. A vase with red flowers. Was she talking about me? It felt surreal, almost otherworldly. I got up to pour myself another cup of coffee, trying to shake it off. But as I turned back toward the living room, my eyes caught the vase sitting directly behind the couch. Red eucalyptus leaves—artificial but vivid all the same. My stomach flipped. I sat down, staring at that vase, my heart racing. *Is this real? Am I in the Twilight Zone?* The skeptic in me wanted to dismiss it, to brush it off as a coincidence, but I couldn't. I'd constantly poked fun at moments like this that defied explanation. But this time, it was different.

I couldn't remember every word she'd said—I was too overwhelmed to write it down—but her message was seared into my heart: *God is working on your behalf. Don't give up. Don't freak out. He's got this.*

What were the odds? *The 700 Club* rarely talked about job struggles—they prayed for the sick, for healing. And yet, here I was, sitting on my couch with those red flowers behind me, hearing exactly what I needed in that moment. It was a faith encounter, plain and simple. God was taking me to the next level, reminding me that even when I couldn't see it, He was working things out.

Not long after that, I got a call from someone outside of Boston. He was a businessman with a farm, bed and breakfast, and restaurant; he needed someone to manage the property and restaurant. He was very interested in me to run this operation. He was a brilliant and kind man who was a World War II veteran and had a super work ethic. We flew to New England to meet in person after a few more phone interviews with his recruiter and son. It was in mid-January and very cold. We met the family and got a tour of the area. They asked me to bring my wife so they could meet her too.

After a couple of days, the owner offered me his car to do some house hunting. I was too embarrassed to ask or admit we didn't have the money for a deposit and rent on a new rental house. The area was drab and old colonial, and the people were not so friendly. But it was better than our current situation, and I would make it work and slap a smile on my face. When you are out of work for several months and feel you are on a downward spiral, you will gladly clean toilets. For some reason, we could not find a house to rent as the availability was tight.

Out of the blue, the owner said we could stay in one of their B&Bs and save some money until the right house opened up. That sounded good to me. We celebrated by going to dinner with one of his staff, who helped show us around the area. On the way home, the SUV died on the highway in the middle of nowhere. It was freezing cold, and there was no cell phone, so my wife and the lady who was with us went to a farmhouse to use the phone to call a wrecker. I stood by the road with a flashlight to prevent cars from hitting the stalled SUV. We returned to the B&B late that night and told the owner and his son about our experience the next day.

They were very apologetic and offered to drive us to Hartford, Connecticut, so we could catch our flight home back to Houston. They gave us a nice check for moving expenses and were excited to have us on board. Full of conversation with them, we narrowly missed our flight home. I was still hoping the Seattle deal would come, as I really didn't want to move to Massachusetts. But I was not about to be picky. If this is what God wants, then who am I to argue?

When we got home, we started making moving arrangements. I called ABF for furniture and car transport to haul one of our cars, as we would drive together in one car. I remember it was about a week or so before we had to move. This gave us some time to say our goodbyes to our church friends, attend a few more services, and say goodbye to my daughters, who were in Houston. I was very choked up about all this, but it was necessary. I called my friend and ex-boss in Dallas to see if the Seattle deal was making any progress. Jack, as I will call him, said there was nothing new to report; I said, "Well, thank you for all you are doing, and I so appreciate the possible opportunity." I told him my wife and I needed to take a position outside of Boston and so hoped that this would have worked out. He understood that I couldn't wait for something that may or may not materialize.

It was Tuesday evening, and we attended our life group church meeting, an offshoot of Lakewood Church. I greatly enjoyed that group, as the people were uplifting and genuine. They would pray for you and stand with you during tough times. A woman who was familiar with South African culture would chat with my wife, and she brought a book with her that evening. She handed it to me and said I think God wants you to have this book. The title was *The New Wine is Better,* written by a South African evangelist, Robert Thom. It was a book on faith—a journey of a man who was an orphan, struggled with alcoholism, and was miraculously changed by the Spirit of God. His faith journeys were so inspiring that they gave me much hope and strengthened my faith. I read the entire book when I got home and have read it several times since. I still have that precious little paperback book; it was life-changing.

Saturday morning, I attended the men's group one last time. I was pretty choked up about leaving. Those meetings were crucial to my spiritual growth. One of the men, an African American brother, said something to me rather loudly as we were engaging with the other men. He said, "Hey, I got a word for you."

"Ok," I said, "what is it?"

He said, "Psalms 37!"

"Psalms 37?" I questioned. "That's it?"

"Yes," he said. "That's it. Psalms 37 is a word for you!"

The group's leader was Steve Austin; I called him the colonel, like in the six-million-dollar man. Steve said, "Well, I guess you will have to read the whole chapter." *Well, alrighty then!* We were starting to wrap up our meeting when another man told a story about moving.

I had not yet told the group where I was going or what my circumstances were; we were just taking a job out of state. He starts by stating he was taking a job in Dallas but did not want to go to Dallas. As he was moving his stuff in the U-Haul, he said he was bawling like a baby. In his long Texas drawl accent, he explained that he did not want to go, "But Lawd, if you want me to go, I will go!" Long story short, he didn't have to move, and as an answer to prayer, he got to stay in Houston. Well, I thought that was amazing! Wouldn't it be nice if I had the same deal?

Monday came, and with it, the ABF container was dropped off at our apartment complex. I offered some cash to my nephew and youngest daughter to help me pack and move. I was getting to the end of the loading, and the tears were flooding. *I'm going to miss my daughter, and I don't want to go to Massachusetts!* I hadn't cried like that since my Junior Village days. I hugged my daughter, promised I would see her soon, and invited her to visit, as the place I was managing had horses and farm animals.

I had one last box to load. It was for my desktop computer; I waited to do this last in case Jack may have some good news in an email. As I went inside to box it up, I checked my email. I did not have much hope because I thought for sure Jack would call first to give me a heads-up.

CHAPTER 8

Exit Stage Left to Mexico

I clicked on my Outlook, scrolled through, and saw an email from Jack. I had to double-check to ensure I had the date correct. The email was written about an hour or so before. It stated, "We purchased the former restaurant you ran in the '90s. Actually, they gave me the restaurant as I was the only one the landlord was willing to put on the lease. I told the landlord you would be the GM and partner. They were thrilled to have you there. We got a great lease deal, and you need to start ASAP! Your position will be COO; we will grow the Pacific Northwest area of other brands. The company is called Seattle Brands." Then, it went on about my salary, bonus, growth 401K, and medical benefits. He would overnight my moving expenses. I would have to handle the formalities with the folks who hired me from Massachusetts.

Stunned, I placed the desktop computer in the box. I was having an out-of-body experience. I went to my wife as she was doing some final packing, and I said, "Guess what? We are going to Seattle."

She exclaimed, "Yes!" We celebrated and embraced with exciting happiness! The ABF trucking company and car transport had no problem going to the left coast from the right. We were now off to Seattle!

With a little extra time, we decided to take the I-10 from Houston to LA and drive up the I-5 to Seattle. When we would gas up the car and take a break, I would take out my Bible and read Psalm 37. Everything in that chapter sang to my heart. Verses like "Wait on the Lord, He will give you the desires of your heart" and "Don't fret" were just a few things I was instructed on, and still, to this day, they are very significant to me.

We arrived in Seattle and began our apartment search. My credit was shot, so finding a good place was challenging without having to pay extra fees and deposits. We finally located a place in West Seattle with reasonable rent and decent proximity to downtown, where I would be working. With a lot of prayers, we made it through the immigration process, and my wife received her green card and the right to work. She found a job working for a dermatologist on the east side, and we were on our way.

We found a great church in Kirkland, WA, and bit by bit, I began to grow spiritually. The teaching at City Church was outstanding. My wife and I got involved in serving as ushers at the Belltown campus and volunteered in various activities, meeting some truly wonderful people along the way.

One friend I made during that time stands out in my memory: Neil, a nephrologist specializing in kidney disease. One evening, after watching a Seattle Supersonics game, we returned to our cars and found ourselves deep in conversation about faith—where we stood spiritually and what we believed. Neil shared something that struck me: he said God had spoken to him, telling him that if he made Jesus the Lord of his life and stopped letting his profession take that place, then God would guide him in every area of his life.

I couldn't help but feel a twinge of envy toward Neil's humility. Here was a man, successful by any measure, who had chosen to place himself under the authority of an unseen God. Despite his intellect and training, he wasn't relying solely on science or reason to navigate his life. Instead, he had embraced a beautifully simple and profoundly wise principle: faith before reason. He trusted that God's guidance was enough.

It might sound strange to some when people say God spoke to them or directed their path. It might seem far-fetched or even naive. But the truth is, God speaks to our hearts in ways that defy human explanation. It's not something you measure or prove—it's something you just *know*. There's a clarity and a peace to it that goes beyond words.

Here's the irony: the enemy, the devil, would much rather you believe he doesn't exist. For nonbelievers, that notion often feels more reasonable—even comforting. But think about it: what better strategy could he have? You won't resist him if you don't believe he's real. And without that resistance, you're left to navigate a chaotic, hate-filled, and violent world armed only with your limited understanding. The result? Confusion, despair, and a life adrift.

Someone once said, "You don't play football using baseball rules." That wisdom stuck with me. Every game has its own structure, its own purpose, and its own guidelines. Life is no different. To understand the purpose of our existence, we must turn to our Creator—the One who designed the game. We can only gain clarity about who we are and what we're meant to do by seeking Him through prayer. Life's rules aren't of our own making—they come from the One who made us.

God, in His infinite wisdom, reaches into the lives of His creation in ways that make sense to each of us individually. He speaks to us in ways we can understand if we're willing to listen. And here's the thing: no one in their right mind would praise or receive blessings from someone they didn't believe in. There's a profound connection between belief and the blessings that follow—a connection that reminds us of the power and presence of God in our lives.

*****

My boss and now partner explained that we needed to change concepts. The reputation of the former restaurant I once ran was not good. So, after several discussions with Jack and the main principal of the Pacific Place shopping center, we decided it needed to be an upscale coastal Mexican restaurant— goodbye, former restaurant Desert Fire, and hello, Mexico. Yes, we named the restaurant Mexico to ensure no one got confused about what type of cuisine we were offering. One thing about Desert Fire: we always had to explain what type of cuisine we offered and the kind of restaurant it was. Mexico fixed that!

Jack entrusted me with the exciting task of hiring an architect and builder! Building strong relationships with architects and builders is essential for any entrepreneur. This opportunity became an incredible learning experience, enhancing my design, budgeting, and scheduling skills. While I'd participated in numerous restaurant openings, this was my first chance to really dive into developing and executing the concept from behind the scenes. I was genuinely grateful for this growth opportunity!

I was in my element, loving every chaotic second of it. With the attention span of a mosquito, I thrived in the whirlwind—keeping the restaurant running, revising plans on the fly, and figuring out how to roll out a new menu and operational strategies. But there was one big problem. I had fired most of the team, including the management. So there I was, working seven days a week, 15-hour days, running on nothing but adrenaline.

When you push that hard, it catches up with you. The fog sets in, and your performance slips. You get cranky and cross. I was spent. I needed help. What do you do in a moment like that? You pray. I prayed, "Lord, please send me someone who can help and bring real value to the team."

And wouldn't you know it? Almost out of nowhere, I got a call. It was from Kevin, a former boss and friend from my Houlihan's days. He'd been an area manager for Jack's old company. Kevin told me about someone looking for a job. Her husband was transferring to Seattle, and she needed work. Her name was Fernanda, and she was, without exaggeration, a godsend. A Culinary Institute of America graduate, sharp as a tack, and a fourth-generation restaurateur.

That's when I realized something else: I was a terrible delegator. In my mind, I thought I was good at it. But God opened my eyes to the truth—I wasn't. I struggled with pride. I wanted recognition. Humility? I didn't even grasp the concept, which was the lesson God was about to teach me.

For years, I'd relied on my experience. I'd opened ten restaurants as a general manager, handled hiring, ran kitchen operations, created recipes, managed costs, knew my way around a bar program, and could hammer out a point-of-sale system like nobody's business. I even had a knack for guerrilla marketing and PR. And yet, for all my know-how, I lacked the two most essential qualities for success: wisdom and humility. Without those, you're just a fog—here for a little while, then gone. God wasn't going to let me stay a fog. He was sanding away my pride, shaping something better, and showing me the power of leaning on Him and others. Little did I realize I was about to get some back-to-basics lessons—not just about running a restaurant but about being a man and a husband. It was a packaged deal, and there was no getting around it.

It started with a review of the menu for the new Mexican restaurant. My partner set up a tasting session with a mix of retail and restaurant pros, the shopping center owner's wife, and a handful of self-proclaimed food enthusiasts. To put it bluntly, the tasting was a complete flop! Even the cheese enchiladas, a dish you'd think would be a safe bet, didn't hit the mark. Ironically, the surprise hit was a salad featuring grilled provolone wedges—something I thought would be a throwaway dish.

The shopping center owner's wife didn't mince words at the session's close. "Carl, better figure out Mexican cuisine, or this isn't just going to fail—it's going to be a financial disaster," she said bluntly. Her words stung. *No pressure, right?* I had thought

I knew Mexican food—after all, I'd honed my skills at Cozymel's with Brinker and at Desert Fire in Seattle. I genuinely loved the cuisine—its depth and vibrancy—but now it felt like I had to start from scratch, step outside of my comfort zone, rethink everything, and find a new approach.

That's when I had an undeniable gut feeling—it was time to appoint Fernanda as executive chef. Fernanda, a classically trained chef, had a deep passion for food but preferred managing the front of the house over being tied to the kitchen. I couldn't blame her for that, but the choice seemed clear. With some convincing, she agreed to take on the role. I devised a plan: she'd continue doing some front-of-house shifts to keep her happy, but her focus would stay on the kitchen. It wasn't perfect, but it felt like the right step forward, one built on awareness and trust.

Our collaboration was seamless; I took the lead on the menu and the language while Fernanda crafted the flavors. Together, we formed a dream team. When we invited the food enthusiasts back for another tasting, a few adjustments from Fernanda left them satisfied, and they gave us two thumbs up.

We began adding managers and building a solid service team. We closed Desert Fire for a remodel that took about six weeks, perfectly timed for the holiday season. This shopping center was ideally situated near hotels, office buildings, condos, apartments, movie theaters, off-Broadway theaters, a convention center, and a museum—perfect for both tourists and locals. All we needed was for the community to embrace our new Mexican restaurant.

There's a saying about starting with the end in mind, and it echoes a biblical truth: write down your vision and make it plain. We named the restaurant Mexico, adding the tagline "Cantina y Vera Cruz Cooking." The idea was bold—a high-end coastal Mexican restaurant highlighting the vibrant flavors of Veracruz and Oaxaca. The menu would feature dishes like fish tacos, seafood enchiladas, and chile rellenos, bringing authentic coastal cuisine to life.

Of course, with any concept, clear financial goals were essential. It wasn't enough to have a vision; it had to be shared with the team. They needed to understand not just the "what" but the "why."

Being in the restaurant business, I knew the balance between hospitality and business was delicate but vital. Lean too far into hospitality, and the numbers wouldn't work. Push too much on the business side, and you'd face declining sales and staff turnover. Success required walking that tightrope carefully—leading with heart but grounded in sound practices.

Jack recognized growth potential in the Pacific Northwest. We met with prospective landlords and developers, allowing me to learn how deals are structured. Sometimes, the best opportunities are the ones you choose to walk away from. Working with developers is a complex process; securing the right location and terms requires perfect timing. If your brand is strong enough, you can be in the driver's seat; if not, it can be an uphill battle.

As the years passed, our restaurant flourished. My wife and I also served as volunteers at our church, working as ushers. At times, it felt more like a security detail, especially given the church's location in Belltown. Occasionally, we dealt with unruly individuals, but we loved being there, particularly during the healing services. Those moments filled me with gratitude for God's immense grace and mercy in my life.

Still, I struggled with pride. It's a subtle and deceptive issue, often cloaked in feelings of offense or an inflated sense of self-worth. Pride can delude you, making you crave attention and recognition in ways that strain relationships—especially with your spouse. When things don't go as expected, it's easy to withdraw or grow distant, unintentionally making others miserable.

I learned this the hard way during an argument with my youngest daughter. She resisted my suggestion to start her homework early. I tried to explain that getting it done sooner meant more free time later and no homework over the weekend—a win-win in my book. She wasn't buying it. The disagreement escalated quickly, and she stormed off to her room. I chalked it up to typical tween behavior. After all, self-discipline and determination are crucial for success, right? Well, partly.

A couple of hours later, I found notes scattered around my study room. The largest one, taped to her door, read, "Stay out! That means you, Dad!" Other notes expressed feelings of being misunderstood and unloved. It stopped me in my tracks. Was all this really over homework?

That's when it hit me: I hadn't taken the time to hear her heart. I'd been so focused on the logic of my argument—what seemed like a practical solution—that I missed what she truly needed from me: understanding, not just correction. Listening to her voice wasn't enough. I needed to listen to her heart.

Taking the time to listen with love brings clarity to any situation. Whether guiding an employee or connecting with your child, the goal is to help them understand your message and see its value. If your reasoning is sound and truly benefits their life or circumstances, you're setting them up for success. But simply lecturing—like when I was in school, where the mantra was "do your homework, no questions asked"—isn't enough.

Telling a cook to go ahead and prepare a piece of Chilean seabass that may be questionable in freshness just because the fish is expensive doesn't inspire their best work. Or refusing to seat a waiter's section because they showed up late—sure, you're making a point, but does it lead to growth? When those moments turn confrontational, and an employee rolls their eyes, it's easy to let offense creep in and think, "I'll show them who's boss." But that mindset serves no one.

Some corporate executives might scoff at the idea of listening with love, brushing it off as something meant for home life, not business. But they miss the heart of what the restaurant industry is all about: serving people with care. At its core, this business is built on principles of hospitality—feeding people, giving them a place to rest, and making them feel valued.

Sure, Harvard Business School will teach you to analyze ROI (Return on Investment) and assess value. But the true secret to success goes far beyond the numbers. The more love we show, the more trust we build with our guests and team members. That trust fosters loyalty, strengthens relationships, and creates a foundation for lasting prosperity. When love leads the way, peace and success follow naturally.

With Mexico Cantina thriving in Seattle, Jack had me connect with a local commercial real estate broker to explore new restaurant opportunities in different shopping centers around the Pacific Northwest. Unfortunately, none of the deals seemed to materialize. Then, one day, Jack secured a restaurant space in the Denver suburbs. It was part of a new outdoor shopping center, which struck me as odd—why build an LA-style center outdoors? But maybe people in Colorado are more resilient to the cold. Jack also developed a steakhouse concept to open alongside the cantina. We were excited about this new venture.

Fernanda and I focused on designing the kitchen and selecting the equipment, aiming to make this project better than anything we'd done before. However, balancing the new opening in Denver with the demands of running a high-volume restaurant in Seattle was overwhelming. Recruiting staff in Denver was tough—we had to hire people out of RVs as we had no space for recruiting, and the labor pool was thin. My big mistake was trying to launch a complex menu with an inexperienced team. Although we opened on time, execution was a struggle. The menu wasn't well received, as the suburban crowd seemed to prefer Tex-Mex over upscale coastal Mexican cuisine. Clearly, our concept wasn't working, and I felt stretched thin between Denver and Seattle.

At home, my wife and I started discussing the possibility of opening our own restaurant. In some ways, I was already doing it—only Jack was footing the bill. Still, I knew I needed to step out on my own. The question was, how?

I floated the idea of buying Jack out of the restaurant, suggesting an owner-financed deal. But the deeper I went into the idea, the clearer it became that I wasn't ready to navigate the complexities of a big lease negotiation. I also proposed we move to a place like Jacksonville, Charleston, or Savannah—cities known for their thriving food scenes. But my wife wasn't on board with relocating to those markets, so we kept praying for clarity.

What we didn't see coming was the recession. The housing market was crashing, and Seattle's real estate was in the middle of a bubble. Home prices were skyrocketing beyond anything we could imagine. In early 2008, we toured a few homes but were talking seven figures, which was way out of reach. I started to wonder if we'd ever own a home in Seattle.

Fernanda, my chef, managed to buy a house in Sammamish for $550,000. But it came with a grueling hour-plus commute one way, and that's in little traffic, which we weren't willing to do. I remember her saying, "Carl, if I don't buy it now, I'll never be able to afford it." I understood her urgency because my wife and I felt the same pressure. We'd paid off our debts, and over the previous six years, our credit had steadily improved. We could afford a mortgage now, but the right house—the one that felt like home—didn't seem to exist. So, we waited, unsure of what would come next.

This brings me to a pressing issue that weighs on the hearts of many small business owners: the real estate market and its ripple effects. The Lord has drawn my attention to places like Seattle, where soaring real estate costs, no tip credits, and rising prices for goods create a perfect storm for restaurateurs. How does one stay afloat in such a landscape?

The Theoreticians

Studies from prestigious universities suggest, in theory, that higher minimum wages stimulate the economy, especially in costly cities like Seattle, San Francisco, and Washington, DC. But here's the hard question: Does raising the minimum wage to over twenty dollars an hour while removing tip credits help small businesses—or hurt them? You can't help but wonder if the policymakers behind these changes have ever run a business themselves. Have they ever had to balance payroll, rent, and rising costs while trying to keep the lights on and the team paid? Or are they so far removed from the reality of small business ownership that they miss the unintended consequences? Let's peel back the layers and take a closer look at what's really happening.

Restaurants in America are more than a trillion-dollar industry—they're the heartbeat of our communities, offering jobs to nearly fifteen million people. But with mounting government regulations, labor mandates, and tax burdens, the future of this industry is at risk. If these trends continue unchecked, the unintended result may be millions of workers forced onto government subsidies, caught in a cycle of dependency that serves no one. Work was never meant to be a handout; it's a gift. There's dignity in earning your way, in being part of something greater than yourself. And yet, heavy-handed policies risk stripping away that dignity, leaving people dependent rather than empowered.

Minimum wage, by design, is a starting point—a stepping stone. It's where teenagers, young adults, and individuals with special needs can enter the workforce, gain skills, and grow.

It was never meant to support a family long-term. The hope is that workers rise above that starting point, adding value to themselves and their employers as they grow. But as wages, real estate costs, and taxes climb, the restaurant industry is forced to adapt. And while restaurateurs are some of the most creative and resilient people I know, these adaptations come with a cost.

With fewer employees and smaller spaces, jobs that used to be stepping stones may start to disappear altogether. The soul of the industry—the vibrant kitchens, the camaraderie of the dining room, the sense of community—could be lost. That's the real danger.

So, where do we go from here? This is a call for wisdom. We don't need Ivy League theoreticians as policymakers. Policymakers must have the common sense to run a small, thriving business in order to balance the needs of workers with the realities of running a business. Restaurateurs and workers alike must continue to innovate without losing sight of what makes this industry vital to American life. Somewhere in this tension lies the solution: a way to allow businesses to thrive, workers to grow, and communities to remain whole. The heart of the industry is worth protecting, but it will take common sense, courage, creativity, and a willingness to listen.

*****

One day, my wife said something that stopped me in my tracks: "I agree. Let's contemplate moving." Her tone was serious yet calm, and I couldn't help but feel a mix of curiosity and excitement. "Where?" I asked, eager to hear her thoughts. She mentioned a place called Rogers, explaining that she thought she'd seen it in a magazine—however, most importantly, she had a dream about it. She wasn't entirely sure where Rogers was, but the name had stuck with her.

Intrigued, I started searching. I searched through the internet maps and directories for Rogers near Seattle, Bellevue, Bellingham, and even as far south as Portland and the Bay Area. But no matter where I looked, I couldn't find any place called Rogers. Nothing fit the description, and disappointment started to creep in. Yet, deep down, I knew my wife's instincts were rarely off the mark. Her spirituality has often led us to unexpected truths.

While driving home across the Alaskan Way Viaduct one evening, I reflected on our conversations about "Rogers." The search had been fruitless so far, but suddenly, as if a lightbulb turned on, it hit me—I *did* know a place called Rogers. But it wasn't in Washington or anywhere near the West Coast. It was in Arkansas. *Arkansas? Surely not!* Memories of my brief stint in Arkansas came rushing back. Years ago, I'd helped open a Mexican restaurant called Cozymel's in Little Rock. I remember one particular evening vividly. A guest and I struck up a conversation, and he asked where I was from. I told him I was up from Dallas, temporarily in Little Rock, to assist with the restaurant opening.

He nodded and said, "Little Rock's okay, but I live in Rogers—God's country. You should visit it sometime." I laughed at the time, saying maybe one day I would. That was back in 1994. Now, fourteen years later, in 2008, this memory came back to me with startling clarity. Could it be? Could Rogers, Arkansas, be the place my wife had dreamed about? That evening at dinner, I shared my revelation with my wife. I fully expected her to hesitate—it was Arkansas, after all, and not exactly the dream destination we'd envisioned. But to my surprise, she didn't bat an eye. Her response—"Let's move away from here"—had a humor to it that reminded me of *The Beverly Hillbillies*, only in reverse.

As if the pieces were aligning perfectly, I realized United Airlines offered a direct flight from Denver to Northwest Arkansas (NWA). The next time work brought me to Denver, I decided to make a quick detour and see this place for myself.

After my Denver visit, I hopped on the flight to NWA and arranged to meet with a local commercial real estate broker. They showed me properties from Fayetteville to Bentonville, but nothing stood out. On my last day there, I decided to take matters into my own hands. I drove around the area, praying for guidance as I explored.

Heading north on Walton Boulevard, I saw a sign for Central Avenue and made a right turn. Both sides of the street were lined with American flags, and I couldn't help but feel charmed by the small-town vibe. As I continued driving, I stumbled upon a charming town square surrounded by historic buildings. I parked the car and wandered the square, taking in the atmosphere. Even with sidewalk construction and barricades diverting traffic, the charm was undeniable. Several "For Lease" signs caught my eye. I noted everything I'd seen and thought *If my wife feels the same way about this place as I do, then this is where we'll move and start fresh.*

Back in Seattle, I shared everything with her, and she was hopeful. A few weeks later, we traveled to Northwest Arkansas together. During our visit, we met Daniel Hintz, a passionate leader working to revitalize downtown Bentonville. As the head of Downtown Bentonville Inc., Daniel was driving economic growth and reshaping the area. He shared valuable insights and connected us with others in the community. Suddenly, the pieces of the puzzle began falling into place.

I called the commercial realtor and asked why he didn't show me downtown Bentonville. He said, "You won't make it there and will probably go bankrupt!" I said I was going to try anyway, and he wished me good luck. Ironically, fifteen years later, he moved his office to downtown Bentonville.

CHAPTER 9

The Exodus

After showing my wife all the properties the real estate agent had taken me to, I saved the best for last—the town square. She loved it immediately. The quaint charm and historic feel caught her attention, and we could both see its potential. This was the county seat, with Walmart's corporate offices just eight blocks away and plenty of vendors in the area supporting the company. But the square itself was quiet, lifeless even, with everything shutting down by 5:00 p.m. We wondered where the dinner crowd would come from. Still, we believed God had guided us this far and trusted He had a plan.

I called a few numbers on the "For Lease" signs scattered around the square. One space directly across from the square caught my eye. Peering through the window, I saw a mess—ladders, paint cans, peeling wallpaper, and debris everywhere. It looked like someone had started a renovation but abandoned it halfway through. It was overwhelming, but something nudged me to make the call.

The banner outside flapped in the breeze as I dialed the number. A gruff voice on the answering machine instructed me to leave a message. I hung up. *No way. This guy sounds like a grumpy old man.* I sat on a park bench with my coffee, debating what to do, when my wife asked, "Are you going to call again?"

I shrugged. "Maybe. Doesn't seem like the friendliest person to deal with." Still, something stirred inside me, nudging me forward. Reluctantly, I stood up and called again. It was another lesson in disguise—that things are rarely as they seem and, sometimes, even less as they sound.

This time, after a few rings, a friendly voice answered. I explained that I'd left a message about the space and sought more information. The voice on the other end said, "I'm heading that way now. I'll meet you in forty-five minutes. I live in Missouri, so it'll take a bit."

We agreed to wait, and I told my wife, "That's definitely not the guy from the answering machine." She laughed, and we walked around the square to pass the time.

A pickup truck eventually pulled up and out stepped a man in jean overalls with a cigarette hanging from his mouth. He headed straight to the building to unlock the door. I turned to my wife and said, "Never judge a book by its cover. This guy could own half the town." We crossed the street to meet him.

The man introduced himself as David and apologized for the mess, explaining that he and his daughter were mid-renovation but had run out of steam. He was friendly and sharp—a man who clearly understood the business side of things. Despite the clutter, we could see the potential: hardwood floors, exposed brick walls, and the charm of a classic small-town storefront. With the proper lighting and decor, it could be a cozy bistro.

After about an hour of discussing possibilities, we stepped outside to reassess the property. Optimism grew as we talked through ideas, but there was a snag. The building only had single-phase power, which was insufficient to support a restaurant. David explained that the breaker panel had about 80 amps, maybe a little more, but we'd need at least 400. He added that new city regulations wanted utility lines underground and we would have to tear up streets or sidewalks to run new lines. I turned to my wife and said, "This won't work."

Just then, as if on cue, the mayor of Bentonville walked by. He greeted David, who introduced us, saying, "These folks are from Seattle and want to open a restaurant in my building, but there's not enough power, and we can't dig up the streets." The mayor, Bob, pulled out his cell phone and called the utility company. Within minutes, he had a solution.

"David, there's a telephone pole in the back alley with three-phase power. They can tap into that and expand the breaker panel." Just like that, the power issue was resolved. The mayor stayed to chat, sharing his vision for the square. "Carl, when we're done, this place will look like a movie set!" His enthusiasm was contagious. With the rent fair and David willing to address a few basic issues, we sealed the deal with a handshake on the sidewalk. Table Mesa was officially born.

Our heads were spinning. One minute, it seemed impossible. The next, everything fell into place. Some might call it a coincidence, but I knew better.

Even with the space secured, doubts crept in. The storefront was small. How would we fit a kitchen, a bar, and enough seating to cover expenses? I told my wife, "If we can just pay the bills, I'll be happy. No more two-hour commutes or driving across two bridges. Fewer people, fewer headaches—this could change our lives."

Later that day, as we sat in the airport waiting for our flight back to Seattle, the questions lingered. How would this work? Could we afford it? Were we making the right decision? Leaving behind my nearly six-year partnership and my wife's secure job at the dermatology practice felt like a gamble. *What if I'm wrong? What if chasing this dream turns out to be the biggest mistake of my life?*

Time wasn't on my side, and I needed divine intervention. But as I reflected on the mayor's unexpected interest in our success and David's support, I realized that God was in this, and that was all I needed to focus on. Like in the story of David and Goliath, I needed to be like David—focused not on the giant but on the God who could deliver me from these obstacles. Now that I think about it, David never referred to Goliath as a giant, only as an uncircumcised Philistine—interesting. In my past mistakes, I didn't have God's guidance, but this time, I did.

*****

As soon as we returned to Seattle, David, the building owner from Bentonville called to tell me that the space next to us had opened up. The tenant had suddenly left for New York City. When he asked if I was interested in leasing it, I immediately said yes! This answered our kitchen and bar space issues—it was all coming together perfectly.

Next, I had to meet with Jack and let him know we were moving to Arkansas. But the doubts came rushing in like a storm. *Are you sure this is the right decision? You're not getting any younger. One more mistake, and you're finished!* The fear gnawed at me, relentless and unsettling. Who was feeding me these thoughts? I had the courage to make this move—but did I have the wisdom and discernment to make the right choice this time?

Even while working at our restaurant in Seattle, with a flicker of faith stirring inside me, I knew I needed a quiet place to pray. I had to ask God for clarity one more time. But it felt like I was pestering Him, asking the same questions repeatedly. *Am I incapable of making a clear decision? Am I blind to what's right in front of me?* Frustrated, I told Fernanda I needed to leave early. She had no idea what I was planning yet, and I knew this would be a shock. I was a partner in the business—it seemed like I'd be there forever.

Once home, I rushed upstairs, grabbed my Bible, and sprawled across the bed. I poured my heart out to God. "Lord, I'm confused. I don't want to mess this up. Is this the right time? Is this what You want me to do?" My mind was racing too fast for any systematic Bible reading, so I did what many confused believers do: I flipped the Bible open randomly, praying for guidance.

My finger landed on 2 Corinthians 6:2 in the New Living Translation (NLT): "At just the right time, I heard you. On the day of salvation, I helped you. Indeed, the right time is now. Today is the day of salvation." I couldn't believe it. The words practically leaped off the page, loud and undeniable. That was my answer—clear, bold, and straight from God. The time was now. Some call it a Rhema word—a specific, personal message from God.

That evening, I showed my wife the passage. She read it, nodded, and together, we knew—it was time to move forward. I emailed my business partner, giving a ninety-day notice to ensure a smooth transition. I had no idea what lay ahead— especially with the economy sliding into recession and the housing market collapsing. In Seattle, though, things still looked stable, almost untouched.

A few days later, I sat across from Jack to break the news. His reaction was sharp and direct. "You're making a mistake," he said. "You're leaving a thriving business to start a small restaurant in *this* economy? This is the worst I've ever seen it. You're taking too big of a risk."

Before, a statement like that from someone as sharp as Jack would have sent me spiraling into doubt. He was the kind of person you listened to—savvy, experienced, and usually right. But this time, his words didn't land. They bounced off me as if I were shielded by something stronger. All I could think about was that verse: "The right time is now." And so, I held onto that promise. The fear and uncertainty might have been there, but so was a deep sense of peace. I didn't need all the answers. I just needed to obey.

I met with Fernanda, and she researched the area for us. I have always thought that if you want to find someone or something, Fernanda can do it. She would have made a great detective! She said that Alice Walton, the daughter of the founder of Walmart, was building a world-class American art museum. I didn't give it much thought as our restaurant was two blocks from the Seattle Art Museum. I handed over the reins to Fernanda, ensuring the business stayed on track. My only regret was Denver, where we hadn't been able to achieve our goals.

CHAPTER 10

The Table is Set

We found a small townhouse in Rogers on our house-hunting trip to NWA. We made similar arrangements when we left Houston, calling ABF and a car transport company to send one of our cars to Rogers, AR. This time, we were leaving Seattle for a place we'd never been.

We said our goodbyes to church friends, neighbors, and the beloved restaurant staff. It was bittersweet leaving the place where I had learned so much about true stewardship. But this time, there was no sorrow in the packing—only joy.

This venture was different. It was a genuine 50/50 husband-and-wife business. My wife left her medical career to step into the role of restaurateur with me. And we had a little companion along for the journey—my wife's long-haired Chihuahua, Furby, whom I nicknamed "The Fur." She immediately bonded with me when my wife and I started dating and became my constant sidekick. The Fur traveled everywhere with us, like our baby wrapped in fur.

We arrived in Rogers, Arkansas, in August 2008, right in the middle of an economic downturn. But just two months later, in October 2008, we opened the doors to Table Mesa. Starting a business during a recession came with unexpected advantages. With homebuilding at a standstill, we found plenty of skilled workers—plumbers, electricians, carpenters, even a CPA, lawyer, and restaurant supply company from Little Rock—all eager for work.

From our savings, we were underwriting the project ourselves. Our budget was tight, so we had to get creative. Bill, our builder, was invaluable as we worked to remodel the space. My wife and I poured ourselves into the project, spending long days hammering away plaster to reveal the original brick walls, painting, cleaning, and doing as much as we could ourselves. With the help of a small team, we laid down vinyl tile. I'll never forget the day we ran into our CPA at Lowe's with 1,200 feet of peel-and-stick tile in our cart. He laughed and asked if we were tackling a small home project. We laughed too, explaining it was for our do-it-yourself restaurant.

One challenge we faced was that Benton County was a dry county, and alcohol service wasn't allowed unless you became a private club. At first, I thought skipping alcohol service might simplify things—less liability and fewer headaches. But after hearing the same question repeatedly—"Are you going to have a bar?"—we knew we had to consider it. Some churchgoers voiced concerns about serving alcohol, but ironically, many of those same people were asking if we'd offer it. We prayed about it and felt peace. God wasn't opposed to responsible alcohol service—only its misuse. With that confirmation, we decided to move forward.

To begin the process, we needed a petition with one hundred signatures. Patti Parks, an employee at Arvest Bank, offered to help. She took the petition with her to the bank and came back in no time with well over the necessary signatures. After that, we needed approvals from the mayor, police chief, county sheriff, and prosecutor.

The process wasn't cheap—ten thousand dollars later, including purchasing a nonprofit entity and hiring a lawyer, we were finally on our way to becoming a private club. We met with the mayor and police chief in person and spoke to the sheriff and prosecutor by phone. Each one gave us their blessing. That sealed it for us—serving alcohol with meals wasn't an issue with God. He knew we'd need this license to make the restaurant sustainable. It became clear that His hand was guiding us every step of the way.

I remember a friend from our church in Seattle asking if I felt guilty about selling alcohol at our restaurant. I thought about it and replied, "Not really." She looked at me like I had two heads. Still, I've come to understand that in the restaurant business, one should serve alcohol responsibly, aim for excellence, and unconditionally guarantee the food and beverages.

Looking back, it's incredible that two city slickers from Seattle opened a restaurant in downtown Bentonville in just ten weeks. The space had no infrastructure for a restaurant, but permitting, licensing, inspections, and construction all came together perfectly. On opening day, with only one practice run, we sent staff to pick up our license in Little Rock and Tontitown for our liquor, beer, and wine order—a seven-hour round trip. When they returned, they were exhausted and needed the night off.

With everything in place, we hustled and stocked the bar and were ready for service. My wife ran the front of the house while I managed the kitchen and bar. I trained the waitstaff on mixing drinks and also worked the line. Fernanda, our friend from Seattle, came down to help us open. She spent a week refining recipes and training staff—she was a godsend. On her last day, before she flew out, we took her to Monte Ne Inn for a chicken dinner. Once she left, it felt like something was missing.

From there, we worked seven days a week, from open to close, shopping for supplies during off-peak hours. Our connection with US Foods in Seattle helped us get corporate pricing. Bill Kimble, a local produce guy, took a genuine interest in our business. Sometimes, I'd catch him in our walk-in cooler, rotating stock and checking if we needed anything. His son-in-law, Chris, was also a great support, and Baxter Smith, our US Foods representative, was a real blessing.

Table Mesa didn't take off overnight—it was a process. I remember hearing people walk in during the remodel, saying, "How long do you think they'll last?" Some said six months, and others gave us a year. But pioneers often have it tough before others arrive. Our first few years were lean, with no income. We even survived the great ice storm of 2008, which shut us down for three days. I remember one cold Friday night in January when we had only three tables of guests. My wife and I looked at each other, wondering how we would grow the business. But when in doubt or in case of emergency, break glass and pray! Prayer pulled us through, as it had many times before. That night, we went from three tables to almost being on a waitlist.

Now, you'd think that finding a church in the Bible Belt of Arkansas would be as easy as pie, right? Back in Seattle, which isn't exactly known for being "churched," we ended up at an excellent faith community with folks who understood what living out their faith meant. But strangely, when we landed in NWA—where you can find a church on nearly every corner— it wasn't so simple. We felt like church hoppers, bouncing from one place to another.

I was getting a new kind of lesson in church involvement. The culture in Arkansas, in some (but not all) churches, seems to run on volunteers. Lots of them! In Seattle, even with our busy schedules, we'd found just enough time on Sundays to serve as ushers. Sometimes, it even felt like we were doubling as security at the downtown campus, but it worked for us. In NWA, though, I didn't feel the same pull to serve that way. Instead, God was nudging us to be faithful givers. We even offered to help a church redesign its logo and signage. God guided us to support churches differently—to learn and observe rather than jump straight into volunteering. It was as if He was saying, "I don't want you to live at church any more than I want you to live at the restaurant. I want you to soak up My Word and grow from it."

I thought back to my friend Neil the doctor. He wasn't called to serve in the traditional ways, but God used him differently, and undoubtedly, he was a generous giver. Did that make him less spiritual? Not at all. I began to see that He was leading me down a similar path. God hadn't called me or Neil to be pastors; He called us to be good stewards, godly fathers, husbands, and leaders in our professions.

Here's something I often think about: why don't we see more successful businesspeople actively engaged in church? Maybe—just maybe—it's because their unique gifts aren't fully embraced. Don't get me wrong—churches need greeters, childcare workers, ushers, security teams, lighting operators, and worship leaders. But not everyone is called to serve in those ways, and that's okay.

Church leaders sometimes forget that it's not about being "spiritual enough." Many business leaders are already walking a deeply spiritual path, navigating the pressures of the world while relying on prayer and Scripture daily. In addition to financial support, their experiences equip them with wisdom, leadership, and insight that could be invaluable to a church. If a church only asks them to volunteer in traditional roles, they might feel out of place, leading to a revolving door of givers who never quite feel like they belong. But if their contributions are welcomed and their talents recognized, they can play a powerful role, quietly shaping and strengthening the church from behind the scenes.

In my view, businesspeople don't need to be front and center every Sunday to make an impact. Sometimes, their greatest work happens in the background, supporting the church in ways only they can, with the unique gifts God has given them.

CHAPTER 11

A Government Agent?

One afternoon, my wife and I were chatting about a regular guest at our restaurant. He came in at least five times a week, and I couldn't help but joke that he either loved our food more than anyone else or had a mysterious day job—maybe even a government agent. Eventually, he introduced himself as Randy, a local businessman with easy confidence. He asked to meet with us, explaining that he was planning to build a new space around the corner and wondered if we'd be interested in opening a restaurant there. The idea immediately intrigued us. Opening an Italian restaurant had always been a dream, and after some conversation, we sealed the deal with a handshake. Randy's approach was more formal than the Landlord David at Table Mesa, but his enthusiasm for our success felt just as genuine.

Here's some advice for anyone considering a lease: be cautious with terms like "build to a white box." It sounds straightforward on paper, but in practice, it's open to interpretation. A white box to one person might mean a clean slate ready for paint; to another, it could mean something barely functional. You might also hear "vanilla shell," which is just as ambiguous. In our case, the white box was more of a warm vanilla shell with a touch of chocolate—but, of course, there were bumps in the road.

By God's grace, I found the wisdom to navigate those challenges, and Randy and I worked together to find solutions that worked for both sides. Over the years, we've done a few more deals together, and our relationship has always felt like iron sharpening iron. Every time, we both come away a little better. He's become more than a business partner; he's a friend I deeply respect.

Like any restaurant venture, though, Tavola demanded hard work and long hours. At Table Mesa, we had been grooming a manager to take over as the general manager for our new Italian concept. Everything seemed on track—until two weeks before we were set to take over the Tavola building. That's when she announced she'd accepted a position managing the restaurant program at Crystal Bridges Museum.

I was furious. It felt like sabotage, a massive monkey wrench in our plans. All I could think was, *How could she do this to us?* I overreacted, fretting over the situation and forgetting the wisdom of Psalm 37, which instructs us: "Do not fret." But fret, I did. Ironically, both Tavola and Crystal Bridges were set to open around the same time—Tavola in August 2011, Crystal Bridges in November 2011.

My wife and I prayed hard for wisdom. We needed a new leader, and fast. Managing both restaurants wasn't an option—I couldn't be in two places at once. I even joked about needing Scotty to "beam" me a general manager. Time was running out, and we had to trust God to guide us through this challenge.

Then, I stumbled upon a résumé that caught my eye. It belonged to a young woman with experience in opening restaurants. She had started at Bubba Gump's as a bartender and worked her way up to manager, joining their opening teams. Her name was Whitney. She seemed perfect—a mix of grit and expertise. It turned out that she was eager to relocate closer to her family, who were moving from Kansas to NWA. Plus, Bubba Gump's had recently been acquired by Landry's, a high-volume operation that aligned with our corporate-style training methods.

Here was the twist: Whitney had initially applied for the Crystal Bridges job! Talk about divine irony. We ended up with the better deal, no doubt about it. Whitney jumped in, and we quickly made up lost ground. Despite the obstacles, Tavola turned out to be one of our best restaurant openings—a brand-new concept with no corporate backing, yet it thrived.

Knowing her love for Italian cuisine, I reached out to Fernanda and asked if she could help. She was thrilled. Not only was her support invaluable, but she also brought family recipes that are still on Tavola's menu to this day.

Tavola was a process, much like Table Mesa. It took about two years before we saw any real financial impact. That seemed to be our pattern. Over time, both Tavola and Table Mesa became like bookends, supporting each other as they were practically next door to one another. Tavola eventually expanded to take over the entire building, offering banquet space for large events. Table Mesa also grew, adding more storefronts with the help of our landlord, David. The Bentonville community embraced us, and we felt incredibly welcomed. Leaders from Fortune Fifty companies would host events and dine at our restaurants—we were truly blessed.

At that point, I was feeling ready for growth. Landlords were reaching out from everywhere, offering spaces to open another Table Mesa or Tavola. Little did I realize I was about to get a hard lesson in humility. Whenever a new opportunity arose, I would pray, "Lord, if this isn't from You, close the door!" It sounds like a good approach, right? And it could be if your heart is in the right place. But mine wasn't, and I wasn't really listening to God. It began to take a toll on my relationship with my wife. I felt like she was always negative, constantly advising me on how to solve the restaurant problems. I thought, *Who is she to tell me what to do? I'm the one with all the experience in the restaurant business, and I brought her into this!* I started getting offended easily and became more unhappy with each passing day, even imagining us going our separate ways. I was blinded by pride, and I didn't even see it.

I thought I had found God, but my work had become my idol. I was deceiving myself into thinking God was hearing my prayers, but they were hitting a brass ceiling. I needed a change in attitude, and I got it—in both my business and personal life. I continued reading the Bible, but it wasn't sinking in. I was turning into what I call a "snork"—a jerk—not the caring, supportive husband I should've been. I couldn't hear my wife's heart when she spoke; all I did was get defensive and think of how to counter her words. But her correction was precisely what I needed, especially when it came from her. Instead, I was avoiding the conflict, mentally perched on the roof to escape the friction. The truth was, I was the problem, and I finally understood Proverbs 21:9: "It's better to live on a corner of the roof than share a house with a quarrelsome wife." New International Version (NIV)

While it takes two to craft the graceful steps of a waltz, I believe that if we husbands can meet life's difficult moments with patience and the art of truly listening—active, Shema listening—God can weave His work into our marriages, restoring the harmony and *shalom* we all long for, even in my case, even with a bit of humor.

In the spirit of Proverbs 21:9, the roof becomes a curious retreat—Yet the wisdom of the Drifters' *Up on the Roof* carries a whimsical truth: you can't retreat to the roof and expect solitude forever—so bring your wife along! I can't help but smile every time that tune dances through my mind.

Now, is learning humility an art you must develop over time? You can't just read a book on "How to Be Humble in 10 Easy Steps"—that would only lead to pride for finishing it and saying, "I finished it in five steps!" C.S. Lewis put it best in *Mere Christianity*:

> If anyone would like to acquire humility, I can, I think, tell him the first step. The first step is to realize that one is proud. And a big-gish step, too. At least, nothing whatever can be done before it. If you think you are not conceited, it means you are very conceited indeed.

The bottom line is, if you think you're humble, you're likely not—you're actually quite proud. True humility comes when you recognize there is someone greater than yourself and acknowledge that. It's in that realization that you begin to experience genuine humility. The Bible says Moses was the humblest man on earth, which is likely why God chose him to lead the Israelites to the Promised Land and be part of the exhibit of incredible miracles, like parting the Red Sea. It's fascinating when you take a moment to think about that!

We decided to open a location in Joplin, thinking we could grow into a big chain, maybe even a franchise! I believed we'd be a great addition to Joplin after the 2011 tornado, offering the community a solid restaurant. We found a great building downtown in the historic district—a cool, classic warehouse owned by a local doctor who had his medical practice upstairs. It seemed like a no-brainer, but I was wrong.

We faced constant challenges—struggling to keep our staff steady and our guests satisfied. Weekends brought a bit of relief, but weekdays were painfully slow. This pattern shadowed us as we expanded Table Mesa to Fayetteville and Conway. Something wasn't right, but I couldn't see it at the time. Looking back, I realize there were flaws in me—traits I hadn't confronted. Pride masked as humility, a stubbornness inherited like a chip off the old block. It was a sobering realization: the last thing I ever wanted was to reflect the traits of someone I'd rather not emulate, let alone be compared to the son of the devil.

One weekend, we were in Branson, MO, and decided to check out a church along 76 Country Blvd. The preacher was giving a message on humility. I thought, *Now, that's a word I could use.* Then, something extraordinary happened. He began speaking in tongues in the middle of his sermon as if caught in a moment of deep reverence. I know that can be controversial for some, but after each unfamiliar word, he'd translate it back to clear English. It was as if he knew exactly what my heart needed to hear. I found myself scrambling for a pen to take notes, wanting to capture every word.

He said, "Many have gone as far as they can go. Unless there is a change in the heart, they can rise no higher." Then he looked out over the congregation, and it felt like he spoke directly to me. "You grew up a rebellious teenager—you couldn't see it because rebellion was all around you. But now your eyes are being opened to the Humble One—Jesus of Nazareth—the perfect Father-pleaser! The meek One!"

He paused, letting the words settle, then added, "The moment the heart changes, the flow of increase begins. Don't undo the favor of the Lord with stubbornness. Don't block His plans for your life with your resistance."

I walked out of that church feeling like I'd been hit right between the eyes with a truth that had been waiting just for me.

CHAPTER 12

Lessons from the Table

A s a believer, it's been a process, but as the saying goes, "A fine wine gets better over time." Slowly, I started to get it, though I sometimes felt like a blockhead. The name of our company should have been the clue I needed. God gave us the name Table for a reason. A table, after all, is where people gather, where meals are shared, and where things are built, little by little, over time. It's a foundation. If I'm meant to be like a table, with things built on me, I need to get flat. I must humble myself, be thankful for what I have, and show grace— especially to my wife. Marriage is a big deal to God—it was His idea—and we all want to see our ideas succeed.

Then, we were blessed with a beautiful daughter. My wife and I weren't sure we'd have more children, as I already had two daughters from my first marriage. And just before our daughter was born, our little Chihuahua, The Fur, who'd been with us for years, passed away, almost like she sensed it was time to make room for a baby who'd soon be toddling after her tail and snout. We missed that precious pup, as she was like a child to us. But soon, our daughter filled that space of sorrow, and for her sixth birthday, we even got her a long-haired Chihuahua, which has been a joy.

I'm still growing in my faith for over twenty years now, but I have a great guide—prayer—and reading God's Word keeps me going in the right direction. It's like using Live View on Google Maps when you tap the walking function and set off thinking you're following the right directional arrow, only to realize you need to adjust to get back on track. My experience with God is that He's a supportive guide through life. He's never written me a check or gotten me out of a jam I created. However, I've noticed that when I'm in a situation where I feel uncertain or resigned to my fate and yield, that's when God shows up.

I could share countless examples of how God intervened in my life long before I set foot in a church. One moment stands out clearly from when I was loosely associated with Jehovah's Witnesses. I was working for an oil service company and driving alone on a cold afternoon on a small county road in the Texas Panhandle. After picking up some takeout for the crew, I was on my way back when an AM radio announcer came on, warning drivers about black ice. I'd heard of black ice before but didn't really know what it was. The announcer urged caution and advised driving slowly. But slow? Well, I didn't know what that meant. I was going 65, maybe 70 MPH, when suddenly, the 1980s Chevy Suburban I was driving slid sideways off the road.

The Suburban veered toward what looked like a cow pasture, heading straight for a massive oak tree. I slammed on the brakes, but it didn't help—in fact, it felt like the truck was accelerating. I wasn't even sure if I had my seatbelt on. All I could see was that oak tree getting closer and closer. In sheer panic, I cried out, "Jehovah, help!" That was all I knew to say—just one thing I'd picked up from the JWs: that God's name was Jehovah.

What happened next felt almost unreal. The next moment, I was back on the road, perfectly aligned in my lane, with full control of the Suburban. The radio was still playing, and when I glanced over, the oak tree was now about a hundred yards away. It was as if none of it had even happened—but I knew in my heart that God's hand had saved me. From that moment on, I slowed down to about 25 MPH.

When I arrived back at the job site, I shared what had happened. One of the engineers offered a scientific explanation, saying that ice can cause a vehicle to accelerate and make you feel like you've lost control. He told me it was all physics and that I just got lucky. I thought about what he said, but deep down, I knew the truth. The moment I cried out to Jehovah, I was saved. There was no coincidence about the timing; His grace spared me.

There are so many stories I could tell—like the time I was saved from drowning while surfing during a winter storm or the dangerous situation when a stranger broke into our apartment when I was a little boy in Washington, DC. But those are tales for another time. For now, this one moment reminds me that God's hand has always been there, guiding and protecting me, even before I truly understood who He was.

I share these moments because they're real, vivid pieces of my life that remind me of something greater at work. Perhaps you, the reader, have had similar moments—those brushes with the astonishing—or maybe you'll dismiss them as happenstance. But here's the truth: there is a God. And the more time we take to seek Him, the more He reveals Himself. For that, I am endlessly thankful.

*****

Life hasn't always been smooth sailing, especially in business. We faced our share of setbacks, but we kept pushing forward. In 2017, we opened Mirabella's Table, an Italian market-style restaurant in Rogers. It took nearly two years to gain momentum, but we began to find our stride. By late 2019, we took on a new challenge: purchasing a property in Bentonville near the downtown square. Suddenly, we weren't just restaurateurs— we were developers. We found ourselves navigating city regulations: building pedestrian walkways, planting specific trees, designing water retention systems, and securing waivers for traffic flow and aesthetics. It was a whole new world, but we pressed on. The result? A cozy neighborhood grill called Table on 6th, where we now serve hearty, crowd-pleasing favorites like burgers, steaks, salads, and fried chicken.

I recall listening to a congressman from South Carolina on the news one day discussing then-President Trump. He candidly remarked that every effort had been made—from investigations to impeachment—to remove him from office. Then he said something that struck me: their next move would be to wreck the economy. This was in the late fall of 2019. Fast-forward roughly six months, and the economy had indeed been severely impacted.

CHAPTER 13

Living on 10%

Then, on Friday, March 13th, 2020, came the COVID-19 orders, and it took no prisoners. Ninety percent of our revenue vanished as if someone just flipped a switch. COVID-19 and the lockdowns brought a whole new set of challenges.

The government started handing out Paycheck Protection Program (PPP) loans, and you could be forgiven if you had the payroll costs to qualify for that. Fortunately for us, we have significant payroll costs. However, the PPP was only good for rent, payroll, and utilities. This did not cover significant things that helped generate an income, like the cost of goods, supplies, and other major overhead expenses. I consider it very providential that this crisis happened to us in Arkansas.

We would have been done for and never recovered if we were in Seattle. Many restaurants on the West Coast suffered from this. It gives you reflection time to be thankful for what you have. In my opinion, it was one of the worst-managed crises we have ever been through as a country. Shutting down schools, workplaces, gyms, parks, churches, and theaters and leaving open places like liquor stores and big corporate box stores was something straight out of a *Blade Runner* movie.

I thought, well, Lord, maybe this is it for us, and our run in the restaurant business has ended. I know our routines will be interrupted eventually, and perhaps this is it for us.

It was as if the Lord gave me a little nudge and seemed to say, "Hold your horses, Slick! Get in there and get to work!" So that's exactly what we did. Suddenly, we were starring in videos that probably made us look like the guy on the used car lot inviting folks down to buy a car for a great deal!—but hey, desperate times, right? We launched what we called "emergency takeout" specials. We were determined to be the fighters on the front lines, ready to compete with grocery stores on price and quality. Our mission? To be part of the solution, not just another problem! And if that meant some quirky marketing and a lot of hard work, so be it!

Now, during that time, all kinds of theories were floating around. A friend of mine in the medical field mentioned that, if the experts were right, wearing masks should have flattened the curve within a couple of months. But that's not what happened. COVID cases climbed, and the death toll seemed to rise even higher. But there was something off about the numbers—it seemed like every death was marked as COVID, no matter the cause. Walk out your door, get hit by an anvil, and you'd somehow be counted in the COVID statistics.

Restaurants were caught in the middle, ours included. Every day brought a new rule—limited hours, outdoor dining only, takeout only, and the looming possibility of shutdowns. If you questioned the city or the state? Get ready for fines or worse.

Here's the thing: if you have faith in a great God who loves you, then you've got something truly extraordinary—something the average person might not have. That "something" is the assurance that, no matter how unpredictable life gets, God holds the final say. You can choose to put your trust in government and experts, and live in a constant state of fear, or you can place your trust in the Almighty to guide you through. His love has a way of driving out fear. Now, don't get me wrong—my wife and I weren't immune to anxiety. We had our moments. But one verse from Psalms kept us grounded: "It is better to take refuge in the LORD than to trust in humans." (Psalm 118:8 NIV). Those words are powerful.

We turned to prayer and anchored ourselves in Psalm 91, clinging to its promises like a lifeline. "You will not fear . . . the pestilence that stalks in darkness." (Ps 91:5,6 NIV) We said those words daily, letting each line bolster us during a time of intense uncertainty. And by God's grace, with faith and patience, we made it through.

When you're walking in spiritual understanding, you've got access to more than just what you can see, hear, taste, or touch. There's a deeper dimension—one that goes beyond human understanding. God isn't limited by human nature; He is spirit, and those who believe in Him must do so in spirit and truth. Trusting in Him keeps you in the light, while falsehood always tries to drag you back into the dark.

Light is a beautiful thing. God created light before the sun, moon, and stars. He created that powerful agent that stimulates sight and makes things visible. How amazing is light! With God in our lives, there is always light and never darkness. We can never pull anything over on Him. I wouldn't have it any other way. All right, I'll stop preaching now—because I'm still a blockhead with lots of growth to go but trust me, this is the kind of wisdom that changes everything.

*****

Here's where it gets interesting: this chaotic time, strangely enough, became a catalyst for us. When restaurants were finally allowed to welcome folks back, even in limited numbers, our businesses rebounded. There was just one challenge—our staff had practically vanished. It was like aliens had whisked away our seasoned employees, and we had to start from scratch, rebuilding with fresh recruits. With time, these rookies grew into seasoned pros, and some are still with us to this day.

Then came the opportunity to buy a local institution. For five years, we had been in talks about acquiring Fred's Hickory Inn—a place deeply woven into Bentonville's history, serving generations of families for over fifty years. In late 2020, during the thick of the COVID era, it felt like the right time. Only God knows when the moment is right. With His guidance and some creative financing, we were able to secure Fred's—a property with strong bones and prime real estate in North Bentonville.

Fred's was crying out for new life. After the original owners passed away, our friend Randy—an accomplished local businessman and our landlord at Tavola—did his best to keep the place running with a few partners. But Fred's needed more than just patchwork solutions. For five years, negotiations had gone back and forth like a carousel ride. Finally, after a last-minute agreement, Fred's Hickory Inn became part of our boutique restaurant family. Once we took over, the big question loomed: Do we preserve Fred's exactly as it was, or do we give it a new direction?

In the end, we did what we do best. We poured the care and expertise of the Table Restaurant Group into Fred's, honoring its legacy while steering it toward the future. That first year wasn't easy. Longtime regulars—especially on social media— were vocal about their displeasure with the changes. Many wanted Fred's exactly as they remembered it from the '70s and '80s. But we stayed the course, striving to balance tradition with progress.

I get it. Change is hard, and nostalgia holds a powerful place in people's hearts. But times were different after COVID. Labor shortages, rising costs, taxes, and real estate challenges shifted the playing field. As much as you want to make everyone happy, you must trust your instincts, pray for wisdom, and make decisions that align with your mission.

Today, nearly four years later, Table at the Hickory Inn (formerly Fred's) performs better than it has in decades. It wasn't easy. As my wife often says, "The tallest tree catches the most wind." At the end of the day, you're responsible for the people you employ, the business you run, and the family you're supporting. That means making tough decisions, sticking to your values, and following the path God has laid out for you.

Social media is a funny thing—a double-edged sword if there ever was one. It's both a blessing and a curse. On one hand, it gives people a voice and a platform to share their thoughts. Conversely, it turns everyone into a critic eager to tell you how to run your business. And while I don't put a lot of stock in reviews, I'd be lying if I said they didn't affect me—or my business.

To me, running a business is a partnership not just between me and the people I serve but between me and God. There are things I can control, and there are things I can't. The menu? That's my responsibility. Training a staff that's skilled, kind, and efficient? That's on me. But the economy? Parking? Road construction? Those are outside my hands. That's where I lean on the Lord. I trust Him with the heavy lifting while focusing on the nuts and bolts of running a restaurant.

Then there are the reviews. You can't control what people decide to write or their mood when dropping that dreaded one-star rating. But as Justin Wilson, the legendary Cajun chef, might have said, "I gare-on tee you'll get good reviews if you pour your heart into creating a high-quality, authentic experience for your guests." That's where I choose to focus—on the part I can control. The truth is that good reviews will always outshine the bad, just as darkness cannot suppress light. Excellence has a way of speaking for itself, silencing the noise of negativity over time.

At the end of the day, running a successful restaurant—or any business—isn't just about the food, the service, or the ambiance. It's about character and integrity. It's about showing up with your best daily, guided by a commitment to serve others well. With the Lord's guidance, I believe those qualities will always shine through. Social media may shape opinions for a moment. However, true success is built on something deeper: a relentless dedication to excellence, an unshakable faith in the people you serve, and the trust that God will handle the rest. Good efforts, grounded in faith and integrity, will always bring success.

CHAPTER 14

Gratitude and Grace

Let me share this vision I had of being thankful and appreciative, which I believe the Lord conveyed in the manner of a parable, as Dickens might have penned it:

Once upon a time, a young orphan girl was taken into the care of a wealthy English family of high standing. The father, a retired officer of the Royal Navy, and his wife, a woman of refined intellect and noble character, opened their doors to this poor child when she was but six years of age. Abandoned and alone on the grim streets of London, she had somehow survived until the good people of a nearby church found her and took pity. Only God knew how long she had wandered, destitute and friendless.

Over time, she settled into her new life, gradually feeling more at ease in her grand surroundings. Yet, in the chambers of her mind, a thought began to fester: that she was somehow entitled to more because she had suffered as an orphan. She perceived her past as an injustice for which she was owed recompense.

Though she lived in a magnificent home in London with every comfort and luxury, she grew dissatisfied. Her room was splendid, with a private balcony overlooking a beautiful courtyard. She had the company of three older adopted siblings, and the family treated her with the utmost care and love, sparing no effort to prepare her for a bright future. She enjoyed frequent outings and trips to the seaside, the finest medical care, and the devoted attention of a private tutor.

But she began to murmur to herself. "Why must I endure all this relentless study? Piano, arithmetic, languages—none of it interests me. I long to dream of distant lands, free from the dictates of others. Why must I rise at a set hour, take my meals punctually, and attend to studies as they command?"

As the years passed and she grew into a young lady of twelve, she expressed her discontent to her adoptive mother and tutor. She declared she no longer had an interest in her studies and would not tolerate being told what to do. With a gentle resolve, the mother replied, "I will discuss this with your father, and we shall give you our answer."

After much deliberation, the father and mother decided the girl needed wisdom that books and tutors could not provide. Summoning her to the parlor, they explained that since she did not value the privileges she had been given, she would no longer reside in the family's quarters but instead in the servants' rooms. With resentment in her heart, the girl turned her back on them and stormed out, moving her belongings to a humble room near the kitchen.

There, she was assigned chores under the housekeeper's watchful eye. She loathed the work and allowed bitterness to grow within her soul. In time, she declared with defiance, "Do with me as you wish, but I refuse to live like a servant! I won't submit to your commands, nor will I return to my studies. Cast me out if you must—I care not, for no one loves me."

So, she was placed in a small, cold room near the front door while her parents sought a solution. One frosty morning, the house cook invited the child to accompany her to the market. The streets were filled with people huddling around barrels of burning rubbish for warmth, families with hollow faces crowding in shop doorways, and beggars crying for alms. As they filled their baskets with provisions, the young girl could not help but gaze at the destitution around her. She wondered, *Why do these people suffer so? What twist of fate left them in such despair?"* Her thoughts lingered on the plight of those less fortunate than herself, and she realized that perhaps they had no choice or control over their fate.

Back in her cold room that night, she lay awake, reflecting on her own choices. She began to see her ingratitude, realizing that a family had opened their hearts and home to her, lavishing upon her every comfort and advantage. Her selfish pride had blinded her to the love they had shown her, and she yearned to make amends.

With the first light of morning, she sprang from her bed, ran upstairs, and cried out, "Father, Mother, my dear family, please forgive me! I am unworthy to be part of this household, but if you find it in your hearts to forgive, I would gladly scrub floors if only to remain here." Her family, filled with compassion, rushed from their rooms to embrace her.

From that day forth, the girl embraced her studies and cherished the love of her family. She grew into a young woman of talent and grace, eventually becoming a celebrated performer, enchanting audiences with her piano and voice. Through this journey, she learned a profound truth: that pride has many faces.

Whether believing yourself to be superior to others or sinking into feelings of unworthiness, both are subtle forms of self-absorption. These thoughts trap and imprison us within the confines of our own minds. True freedom comes when we take these thoughts captive and replace them with truth. Real strength is found in humility and obedience—in looking beyond ourselves to recognize, yield, and embrace the goodness in others.

Here is some wisdom for the future Restaurateurs: And here in Bentonville, where new businesses are springing up like flowers after rain—modern offices, boutique hotels, and restaurants lining the downtown street—it's clear our town is thriving. We were one of the few dining spots for years, but now we're part of a vibrant culinary community. All this competition can feel a bit threatening, even nasty at times, but that's where faith steps in. God calls us to pray for the prosperity of our whole town, and when we do that, we're planting seeds for everyone's success. A thriving town brings opportunity to all, especially those who serve their community with dedication and vision.

If God has placed you somewhere, you don't have to worry about the competition. He gives you the vision and the purpose, yes, anointing full of God, and it's up to you to run with it. As Jeremiah 12:5 reminds us, "If you have raced with men on foot and they have worn you out, how can you compete with horses?" (NIV) This isn't just a business; it's a calling, a chance to rise to the occasion and build something that brings lasting value to those around us. No one can lay claim to every corner. In this industry, it's about resilience, staying sharp, and having the endurance to overcome challenges and relate to the team members you hire.

I've seen plenty of brilliant people close their doors, not because they lacked skill or resources but because they couldn't or wouldn't keep up with the long journey ahead. Running a business means going back to the basics every day. Vince Lombardi once gathered his players, held up a football, and said, "Gentlemen, this is a football." Sometimes, amid ambition and growth, we need that same grounding. In the restaurant business, whether you're serving gourmet meals in a Michelin-star restaurant or comfort food in a shack, it always comes down to the basics: cooking, cleaning, and serving—hopefully with excellence and heart.

When it comes to growth, it's about more than just landing that prime location. Sure, location can help, but I've seen little "hole-in-the-wall" places succeed because they pour love and care into every detail. My mother used to say, "People are fickle and feeble-minded; they'll stay loyal right up until something shinier catches their eye." And a lawyer friend once joked that loyalty lasts only until the "next speed model rolls in." But here's what I know: if there's real love behind what you do, people feel it and keep coming back. It's not easy, and it often means operating on slim margins and giving your all day in and day out, but it's worth every moment. Succeeding in this business requires more than skill. It requires faith, resilience, and the willingness to "run with the horses."

When I read Psalm 23 and came to the line, "You prepare a table before me in the presence of my enemies," I felt God saying, "I am with you. Don't worry about the other players; focus on the banquet table I've set before you." When God anoints and fills you with Himself for a task, it is as though He has poured a special assuasive oil over you. It's His way of showing you that you are the one chosen to be here and now and that you have been granted the ability to complete the assignment. Faith gives you the courage to stay on course, even in the face of rivalry.

That moment sealed it for me—finally understanding the meaning behind the name of our business after so many years. Isn't it funny how you can go decades without grasping something, or maybe it's just God's way of slowly revealing His gifts for us? I remember when I lived in Houston, and I used to drive past this enormous billboard that looked like a giant gift box with a bow. Each week, the ad company would peel back a small part, revealing just a hint of what was inside.

For months, I joined thousands of other drivers, wondering and guessing what it could be. When it was finally unveiled, it turned out to be a new hospital on the west side of Houston. That billboard kept people curious, drawing them in little by little. And you know, I think God works a lot like that with us. He reveals His plans in pieces to keep us curious and moving forward. Maybe our minds can't quite handle everything He has in store all at once.

I must have read Psalm 23 countless times, but on that special day, as I read, the line about "preparing a table in the presence of my enemies" seemed to jump off the page and settle deep in my heart. Suddenly, it had a new meaning. I'll never look at a table the same way again.

Even when competitors spring up around you, remember that their ambitions might not align with yours. If you want to grow, open another location, and make a name for yourself, prepare for a steep, uphill climb. But if you're following a path set by God, with your heart tuned to His direction and a touch of His anointing, then your journey is entirely different. Don't chase after every trendy development just because it seems lucrative—it often costs more than it's worth.

And don't feel slighted if you don't see your name in prominent restaurant publications or land a James Beard nomination. I've dined at some of those "acclaimed" spots and left wondering what all the fuss was about. I even remember a well-known chef stopping by my Seattle restaurant, casually saying he just needed a snack before catching a movie across the street. Some of these "celebrity" chefs make their rounds, supposedly giving restaurants a shot at "making it big." But what does "making it big" really mean? Bragging rights? Recognition from the right people?

A Seattle Times critic once described our place as "not bad for mall food." Did it sting? A little. But it taught me something. Those "prestigious" restaurants with glowing reviews in the trendiest neighborhoods? Their sales were often mediocre. Meanwhile, our so-called mall food was pulling in four times the volume. Guess who was smiling all the way to the bank?

We're seeing a similar pattern here in Bentonville. So, if the glossy publications aren't noticing you, don't sweat it. Ask yourself: Who am I really trying to please? And strive for excellence, stay true to your moral compass, and wish your fellow restaurateurs well. That's where the real success lies.

You've probably heard this before: "It's just not a fit, or you're not a fit." Maybe you've heard it about your child at school, yourself at work, or even at church. "You just don't fit in here."

But honestly—who really fits in anywhere? And what are we supposed to do to fit? In my view, the answer is simple: nothing. We're all uniquely different, each of us bringing our own talents and skills to the table. The sooner companies, schools, and churches understand that, the stronger and more stable their communities will be.

It's a real issue in the church. People move from place to place, saying, "I'm not getting fed." They're looking for the perfect meal but forgetting that feeding yourself is also part of spiritual growth. And I've seen good folks asked to leave a church for being too outspoken. But if church leadership can't handle a little feedback or suggestion, it may be time for some soul-searching. As believers, it's essential to approach things with humility, but a healthy church should also be able to handle honest dialogue.

I'm not the kind to charge up and hand the pastor my opinions unless I feel genuinely led. And even then, it's usually something simple—offering support for a project, not a full-blown critique. Sure, I might grumble to my wife about a service running long, my attention span being what it is, but that's just human nature. That said, when a message is genuinely gripping and soaked in truth and relevance, you'll find me hanging on every word, no matter how long it lasts. Good teaching grabs hold of you like that.

Pastors carry a heavy responsibility—to feed the flock and act as undershepherds. It's their calling, but it doesn't mean the rest of us get to sit back passively. If you're serious about growing in your faith, start with the basics: open your Bible daily and feed yourself. Seek out trusted teachers and pray for discernment. And when something doesn't feel right, compare what's preached to the Word of God. In Matthew 10:16, Jesus told us to be as shrewd as serpents and as innocent as doves. That includes being discerning, even in church.

As for being "too churchy"? Genuine faith has never been about appearances or theatrics. I learned that early on. When I was part of a men's prayer group at Lakewood Church, I stood next to a sharp and polished guy who could deliver the perfect "blessed and highly favored" line like a pro. I'll admit I felt a bit intimidated. He sounded so holy, so put-together. But then, a few weeks later, he disappeared. When our leader asked about him, we discovered he'd been arrested. Turns out, the man was battling a serious addiction that had landed him in jail. At first, in my so-called newbie Christian mindset, I thought, *Well, that'll teach you to act all high and mighty.* But the truth hit me harder than I expected: the people who seem to have it all together often carry the heaviest burdens. It was humbling—and a sobering reminder that I still had a long way to go. Truthfully, I wasn't all that far from that man's struggles.

At its core, God calls us to authenticity, not perfection. He doesn't want a flashy faith; He wants something real. He's our refuge and our safe place, the shadow under which we find the strength to face life's hardest moments. The church isn't about who's more polished or who looks the part. It's about showing up, leaning into the strengths God gave you, and doing your part in the mission. It reminds me of the military. Parents might encourage their sons to enlist for the structure or discipline, which isn't bad. But the military doesn't want people just looking to blend in. It needs people who are ready to serve, period. And if you make it through, you walk away with lessons in loyalty and camaraderie that stick with you for life.

Jesus said, "Greater love has no one than this: to lay down one's life for one's friends." (Jn 15:13 NIV) But laying down your life isn't just about risking your physical safety. It's about stepping outside your own world, shifting your focus to others, and serving in ways that often go unnoticed. That's the kind of love that matters most—that makes a difference where it counts.

I learned this when my daughters faced challenges at school or activities —feeling left out, even bullied. It cut deep. My first instinct was to storm in, fix it myself, and set things straight. But would that really help? I knew better. Anger doesn't heal anything; it just throws fuel on the fire. So, what's the high road in situations like this? It's not about ignoring the problem or turning the other cheek blindly. Jesus taught a deeper, more lasting way—a strategy that begins in the spirit before it manifests in the physical. I like to call it "Operation Jesus." Picture Psalm 23: even in the valley of the shadow of death, you're not alone. God is there, comforting and guiding. Psalm 35 reminds us to ask the Lord to contend with those who contend with us, trusting that He sees every heart and every angle of a situation.

This isn't just about a dance studio. That little period when my daughter struggled, mirrors what so many of us face in life and business. There are lawsuit bullies, city officials bullies, employees who make choices that hurt the whole team, and customers who forget basic respect. I've had moments in the restaurant where celebration turned to chaos in the blink of an eye. Life doesn't come without conflict. But faith reminds us that every challenge is a chance to lean into God's strength and let Him handle the battles we can't fight on our own.

Allow me to share a restaurant experience, one that has all the twists and turns of a Mark Twain tale. Since I've been immersed in the works of classic writers lately, it seems only fitting to imagine how the man himself might have told this story—with his signature blend of wit, grit, and heartfelt observation of the human spirit.

Once upon a time, there lived a little old lady in Dallas—a woman with a backbone of iron and a spirit sharp enough to skin a mule. With a conviction that brooked no argument, she had resolved to host a graduation party of such grandeur that folks would talk about it for generations. The guest of honor? Her grandson, a lad who had managed to escape the clutches of academia and, by the grace of God or his own cunning, had finally graduated.

To commemorate this most noble achievement, she selected our humble establishment as the setting for her triumph. Guests, she declared, would be arriving from the far-flung edges of the map—from east and west, north and south, as if summoned by Gabriel's trumpet. The event, in her mind, would challenge Solomon's Temple.

Well, we prepared. Oh, did we ever prepare! The dining room shone like a new penny in the sun—tables set, linens straight, flowers prim and proper, the whole affair polished to Southern perfection. The menu was discussed, agreed upon, and repeated back so many times that even a parrot could've recited it: "Family style, ma'am." That meant plates passed politely, dishes shared, and food served with the dignity befitting fine company.

But as any man knows, the devil delights in miscommunication. To the dear lady, "family style" was a synonym for "buffet"—a sprawling, endless banquet of food where guests might heap their plates to the ceiling and return for seconds, thirds, and fourths if the Lord so willed it.

And then—then came the kinfolk. Not a mere hundred guests, as first planned, but an indeterminate multitude. It seemed half the state of Texas had been summoned, cousins and neighbors spilling through the door like cattle through a broken fence. The dining room groaned under the strain, the waiters sweated bullets, and the little old lady's face soured like milk left in the sun.

We scrambled, I'll tell you that. Plates flew. Adjustments were made. By God's mercy, the guests ate, drank, and made merry. They laughed, they chewed, and at last, they went on their way fat, happy, and none the wiser. But the matriarch—oh, no—she was another matter entirely. To her, the evening had been nothing short of the Titanic, and we were the iceberg. Her imagined buffet never materialized, and her vision fell to ruin. Though her guests departed grinning, she clung to her disappointment as if it were her most cherished possession.

From that day forth, she told the tale wherever she went, spinning it with the gravity of a lead balloon. "Ah, yes," she would sigh, shaking her head for effect, "the day they ruined my grandson's graduation." And so, what began as a misunderstanding grew into a legend—her legend, mind you—repeated far and wide, and always at our expense. Such is the way of expectation, friends. It grows mighty in the mind, and when it topples, the crash echoes for all eternity. As the famous saying goes, in the restaurant industry, facts are negotiable, but perceptions are not!

This experience, while slightly enhanced for the sake of storytelling, is emblematic of my industry. In moments like these, I rely on the "measuring rod of truth." I ask myself: "Was I transparent in my dealings? Did I act with integrity?" If the answer is yes and I find myself unfairly accused, the next step is clear—go to the One who handles injustice best. Psalm 35 captures this plea with startling clarity:

> O Lord, oppose those who oppose me.
> Fight those who fight against me.
> Put on your armor, and take up your shield.
> Prepare for battle, and come to my aid.
> (Ps 35:1-2 NLT)

It's a powerful reminder that being a believer doesn't mean being a doormat. Kindness often gets mistaken for weakness, but God's kindness is steeped in strength and unwavering conviction. Yes, He's patient and compassionate, but He doesn't turn a blind eye to wrongdoing or let people skate by without accountability.

Romans 2:3-4, as paraphrased from The Message Bible, puts it plainly: God isn't duped by excuses or finger-pointing. He sees past every defense, straight to the heart. His love is purposeful—not to let us continue in comfortable habits but to lead us to real change. As believers, we are called to embody strength with purpose. True kindness isn't weakness; it means setting clear boundaries, speaking truth with love, and holding others accountable. It's about standing firm in conviction while extending grace—mirroring how God deals with us. No matter the challenge—difficult guests, legal hurdles, or HR conflicts—trust that God will fight for those who seem least likely to prevail. In Him, even the underdog can overcome.

When I look at our seven restaurants—and now an eighth, A1A Table, on the way—I see evidence of a vision far greater than ourselves. We've stayed rooted here in NWA because this is where we're meant to leave our mark. If growth comes, it'll happen on God's timeline, not ours.

Now, you can have the most incredible ideas for a restaurant, but without the right people to bring them to life, they'll remain dreams on paper. A wise mentor once told me, "You can have the best food in the world, but if you can't sell it, you're just sitting on it." From the outside, opening a new business might look glamorous. But from the inside? It's a chaotic storm of heartache, opposition, and endless trials. I think of Jesus's command to pick up our cross and follow Him. What did He mean by that? He was asking, "Are you ready to go all the way, even if it costs you everything?"

Building a team isn't like sending people into battle—though some days, it feels that way. Every team member, from the dishwasher to the general manager, must align with the vision. Personal ambitions must take a backseat to a shared goal. Each person becomes a "disciple" of leadership, working toward a greater mission. It's the leader's job to cast that vision, to connect daily efforts to something bigger and more meaningful. Leadership isn't about barking orders; it's about charting a course, providing tools, and keeping the mission on track. Finding the right leaders takes patience, discernment, and a sharp eye for integrity. Is their life stable and strong? Do they make sound decisions? Good leaders don't just strengthen themselves; they lift the whole team.

And let me say this: a degree doesn't make a leader. I should know—I'm a college dropout. Some of the most outstanding leaders I've worked with didn't have polished résumés or fancy credentials. What they had was grit, determination, and a willingness to learn. Look at Bill Gates or Steve Jobs. Success doesn't come from a piece of paper—it comes from the right mindset and sheer tenacity. Take Milton Hershey, for example. He failed at his first apprenticeship as a printer but went on to revolutionize the world of chocolate. Failure wasn't his ending—it was his launching pad.

In the hospitality industry, I've seen fresh graduates—whether from hotel management or culinary schools—struggle with the demands of real-world leadership. Many want to skip the trenches and leap straight to the top, but skipping the hard work often leads to frustration. Of course, there are exceptions. Our friend, Fernanda, is a Culinary Institute of America graduate who excelled because she embraced the grind and built her leadership one brick at a time.

Here's the truth: leadership requires rolling up your sleeves and being willing to walk alongside your team. This can be an expensive lesson for new restaurant owners, especially those from other industries. I've seen tech moguls and retail giants try their hand at restaurants, only to see their dreams shutter within two years. The mistake? Underestimating the industry's demands.

Hiring a restaurant consultant can be a toss-up. I may suggest taking the time to work in the field, which can save a fortune in the long run. It's an investment in wisdom—a small price to avoid costly missteps. If you're serious about starting a restaurant, shadow experienced leaders, study successful operations, and be willing to start from the ground up. It might mean taking a pay cut or stepping into an entry-level role. But the insights you'll gain will be invaluable. In the end, knowledge isn't just power—it's survival.

If you're already in the business, you've likely learned a few things that can save you time, money, and sleepless nights. I have learned from my corporate experience a concept that breaks business growth into three key phases:

1. The Entrepreneurial Phase

This is where the chaos begins. You're filled with energy and big ideas, pushing forward with all the excitement of a fresh start. But the reality? It's messy. You're operating on instinct, figuring it out as you go. Maybe you've got a good handle on your costs, a sharp-looking staff dress code, and a trendy menu, but it's like trying to fill a leaky bucket. Effort goes in, but results spill out. This is why so many restaurants don't make it past those critical first three years—the leaks don't get fixed. Your job is to find and plug them early, whether that's poor cost management, untrained staff, or unreliable vendors. Build your foundation, or you won't have a structure to grow.

2. The Operational Phase

Once the leaks are patched, it's time to create order. This is where you establish systems and structure. Training manuals, recipe books, quality checks, vendor partnerships—it all comes together to create consistency. Think repetition. Think discipline. This is the phase where "doing it right" becomes second nature, much like Forrest Gump assembling his rifle over and over. Your team needs to operate like that: focused, reliable, and unified in purpose.

To build this team, respect is your cornerstone. Younger staff? Treat them like siblings—guide them with patience. Older staff? Treat them like mentors—value their experience. Disrespect will kill your culture faster than a bad Yelp review. A safe, positive work environment isn't just good practice; it's your responsibility. Professionalism and respect should flow between every team member, creating a culture where excellence thrives.

3. The Strategic Phase

With the chaos tamed and operations humming along the big question becomes growth. But growth without strategy is just a bigger mess waiting to happen. Think of great leaders like Alexander the Great or Napoleon—conquerors who knew that their armies were only as strong as their supply lines. Expansion works the same way. Don't jump into that shiny new spot in Miami when your home base is in NWA. Distance can kill a business.

If you're ready to expand, keep new locations within a manageable range—50 miles is ideal. If you're eyeing a farther market, like Tulsa, which is about 115 miles away, consider opening multiple locations within a small radius there. That way, they can support each other, and you keep logistics tight. And here's a pro tip: if you're traveling often to check on a location, make sure it's a city you enjoy visiting.

But the foundation of growth? A strong labor market. You might find the perfect location in Aspen or Boca Raton, but if there's no workforce to staff it, you're doomed before you begin. A lack of reliable labor or an unaffordable lease will sink even the best restaurant. So, prioritize those two factors above all else: a lease that makes financial sense and a labor market that can sustain your vision. Without them, you're building on sand.

*****

Growth is exciting, but it's also a test of wisdom. Know when to hold back, when to push forward, and how to build something that lasts. With strategy, respect, and faith in the process, success isn't just possible—it's inevitable.

Since moving here in 2008, we've been blessed with seven locations. Given what the restaurant industry went through with COVID-19, this growth feels nothing short of a miracle. It's a testament to resilience and to the way simple things—like a loaf of bread—can bring comfort, connection, and joy, even in the hardest times.

There's an ancient proverb that says, "Know the condition of your flocks." It's a reminder that success doesn't come from neglect; it comes from vigilance and care. Whether it's a flock of sheep, a team of people, or a restaurant, the principle is the same: if you're not tending to what you've been given, things will naturally fall apart. It's like the law of thermodynamics— everything drifts toward chaos unless you step in and do the work.

In the restaurant business, that work goes far beyond checking numbers on a report. It means stepping out of the office and onto the floor. You tighten screws on a wobbly table. You recalibrate ovens that are running too hot. You sharpen knives, replace broken equipment, and—most importantly—you connect with your team. Numbers may give you data, but the heartbeat of any business is its people and processes.

And let's be honest—this industry isn't for the faint of heart. There's no such thing as "day trading" in restaurants. It's not about quick fixes or trendy ideas. Everything, from the food to the culture, requires constant attention. The saying, "If you've got time to lean, you've got time to clean," captures the spirit perfectly. It's relentless, unglamorous work, but that's where we make it happen.

For those willing to embrace it, running a restaurant is like a never-ending adventure—equal parts herding cats and fixing a machine. Yes, it's exhausting. Yes, it feels like there's always one more thing to do. But it's also deeply rewarding. You're not just running a business; you're building something enduring. The financial returns are there, but the real reward comes from the satisfaction of creating a place where people gather, connect, and celebrate life. And in the end, that makes all the effort worthwhile.

EPILOGUE

Isn't it fascinating that Jesus marveled at the faith of two non-Israelites? The woman who reasoned that even the dogs eat the crumbs from their masters' table and the centurion who said, "I'm not worthy for you to come under my roof—just say the word, and it will be done." These weren't the expected faithful; they weren't the ones who grew up with the promises of God. Yet, they believed with a clarity and conviction that moved mountains.

Now, think about this: if a kid raised on the streets of Washington, DC—with a single mom, no father, no breaks, and barely surviving at the poverty line—can grow up in a run-down garage apartment in Jacksonville Beach and still find success through the grace of a heavenly Father, then truly, anyone can. It's not about where you start. It's about who walks with you along the way.

A wife who believes in you, champions your dreams, and stands beside you is one of life's greatest treasures. Every man needs a partner who inspires his mind and uplifts his spirit, someone who breathes courage into his heart when the world feels heavy. This kind of relationship is more than a blessing— it's a cornerstone. It lays the foundation for a life built on hope, resilience, and the audacity to keep dreaming big, no matter the obstacles.

Building a business—or pursuing any dream—isn't meant to be an endless grind. It's a journey filled with moments where creativity and joy intersect with challenges and grit. Remember the wild ambitions we had as kids? Back then, nothing felt impossible. So, why do we lose that spark? It's time to reclaim that sense of wonder and possibility. Obstacles will come, no doubt, but here's what I've learned: when we trust God, the right people and opportunities show up exactly when we need them. That's the beauty of divine timing—it reminds us that our potential, through Him, is limitless. Together, we're capable of creating not just success, but lives rich with meaning and fulfillment.

The truth is, we're often our own worst enemies. There are times when we need to be corrected, humbled, even rebuked, which is why Scripture is so essential—it's our compass when we've lost our way. Chapter 6 of Galatians teaches a simple yet profound truth: we reap what we sow. If we chase selfish ambitions, take shortcuts, or let impatience lead us, the harvest will be one of regret. But if we live to please the Spirit—with hearts of humility, patience, and compassion—steady and faithful, we will reap something eternal. That kind of harvest not only helps us endure injustices and challenges but also shapes us into the people we're meant to be.

As I read Exodus 15, one scene stopped me in my tracks. The Israelites—fresh from watching God part the Red Sea—were walking through the wilderness, and their faith hit a wall. Bitter water. No way to drink it. And like clockwork, the grumbling began.

I get it. Water is survival. And when you're traveling with millions, the stakes are high. But here's what floors me: these same people had just seen the impossible. They had witnessed God crush their enemies and rewrite the laws of nature. You'd think they'd pause and say, "If He can split the sea, surely He can give us a drink."

Instead, they doubted.

Then God, with a patience I can barely fathom, steps in. He tells Moses, "Throw this piece of wood into the water." Moses obeys, and the bitter water becomes sweet. Clean. Refreshing.

But it wasn't just about the water. God used the moment to teach them something deeper: *"I'm testing you,"* He said. *"If you listen to Me, if you obey My ways, if you trust Me—not just when it's easy, but always—then I will take care of you. I'll protect you from the diseases you saw in Egypt. I am the Lord who heals you."*

It's a stunning promise, isn't it? A God who doesn't just provide but heals. Who transforms bitterness into sweetness. And here's what struck me most: this wasn't just about their bodies—it was about their hearts. Their minds. Their trust.

So, I started to wonder: does this promise extend to us? To the struggles we face today—cancer, anxiety, diabetes, depression? Could it be that God is still the Healer, working from the inside out? Medicine fights from the outside in, but God's way starts in the soul, renewing the mind and spirit, which in turn affects the body.

I know this idea might feel too good to be true. It might even hurt if you're carrying pain or have lost someone you love. But what if—just what if—we leaned into His promise with childlike faith? What if we trusted Him fully, even in the wilderness?

As for me, I'll take Him at His word.

My Prayer:

Lord, I fall short. I've stumbled, disobeyed, and relied on my own strength when I should have leaned on You. Yet You've been patient, kind, and merciful. Thank You for blessing me far beyond what I deserve.

Father, guide me. Lead me to the place where obedience, wisdom, and truth dwell—not for my glory, but for Yours. Teach me to listen. Help me to trust You fully and do my part no matter how bitter the water seems. I pray that everyone reading this might receive Your blessings—health, strength, and wholeness—just as You've promised.

In Jesus' name, Amen.

www.ingramcontent.com/pod-product-compliance
Lightning Source LLC
Chambersburg PA
CBHW021648120626
46545CB00002B/758